Shaping the Church's Educational Ministry

A MANUAL FOR THE BOARD OF CHRISTIAN EDUCATION

Kenneth L. Cober

JUDSON PRESS®, Valley Forge

Contents

Introduction

THIS MANUAL is intended for use in churches with boards or committees of Christian education, and also in churches organized on the basis of a single board covering all phases of the church's life and work. It may well be studied in corporate sessions, each group determining if and how it will use the ideas presented. It may also be used for personal reading and study.

Shaping the Church's Educational Ministry is a blend of the old and the new. It is a successor to *The Board of Christian Education at Work,* by Clarence B. Gilbert, and as such preserves time-tested ideas and values. It also includes new trends based upon the Cooperative Curriculum Project and other recent developments in Christian education.

Although a church may have a board of Christian education, it does not necessarily follow that the board is functioning adequately. Some churches have a board in name only — a paper board — and most boards could greatly improve their effectiveness. That is the reason for this manual: to help every church achieve its maximum potential in the further development of its educational ministry.

Section 1 | Historical Perspective

THE BOARD of Christian education has a relatively recent origin. It was not until the early part of the twentieth century that churches began to form church-wide committees or boards of Christian education. Since then the number has steadily increased, and today the church without such a board is the exception.

Our curiosity may well prompt us to ask, "If the churches did rather well in the nineteenth century without boards of Christian education, why do we need such a board in the twentieth?" A brief review of our heritage may be helpful, for some churches are still hampered by conditions which have their roots in history.

THE RISE OF PUBLIC EDUCATION

In colonial times, the churches had no need for boards or committees of Christian education. All education was religious education. The content of textbooks was moralistic, biblical, and theological. The teacher was usually the local clergyman, or someone whose competence and orthodoxy he certified. Colonial schools were essentially church schools.

When the colonies formed themselves into an independent nation, they wrote into the Constitution the principle of the separation of church and state. State after state subsequently adopted legislation prohibiting the teaching of sectarian religious tenets in tax-supported public schools. This was the beginning of a movement toward removing religious content and practice from public education which culminated in our own day in the elimination of compulsory Bible reading and prayer from public schools. The separation of church and state demanded a division of labor: the state was to teach "secular education" and churches were to provide "religious education."

The Roman Catholic church, to discharge its responsibility, developed a system of parochial schools which paralleled public education from the primary grades to the university. Criticizing the public schools for being "godless," the Catholic church urged its parents to send their children to Catholic schools. For this privilege, Catholic parents paid tuition for their children's education while supporting public schools through taxes.

DEVELOPMENT OF THE SUNDAY SCHOOL

For the most part, Protestant churches did not choose to create parochial school systems. Instead, they borrowed from England the idea of teaching religion on Sundays. Robert Raikes had initiated a system for teaching the poor "ragged children" who were employed in factories during the week and for whom Sundays offered the only time for educational opportunities.

Several Sunday schools were established in America before 1800. During the next quarter century, the schools increased with great rapidity, even though there was opposition. For some, the Sunday school was a violation of the Fourth Commandment, a desecration of the sabbath. There were pastors who inveighed against the Sunday school as an instrument of the devil and refused to allow classes to meet in their church buildings. Interested laymen often conducted Sunday schools in their homes, in barns, and in other places outside the church meetinghouse.

At the start, the Sunday school was an interdenominational movement. The founders of the first Sunday school society, in Philadelphia, were Bishop White, Episcopalian; Matthew Carey, Roman Catholic; and Benjamin Rush, Universalist. The Baptists and Methodists were among the first denominations to champion the Sunday school movement, followed by the Presbyterians.

As time went by, the Sunday school was accepted by the churches and was permitted to meet in church buildings on Sunday afternoons, or on Sunday mornings before or after the regular worship service. It remained

a lay movement, manned and administered by laymen. Some pastors took an active part in promoting the Sunday school program, while others felt threatened by it. There was a fear that it would compete with the established church program, and this fear was not entirely unfounded.

The church and the Sunday school became parallel and often competitive organizations. Considerable power became vested in the superintendent who was tempted to guard jealously his official prerogatives and might or might not cooperate with the pastor and the total church program. The superintendent personally conducted the Sunday school assembly, which in some respects resembled the church service, with worship or at least an opening exercise and a brief "sermon" which he delivered. He had his own program, his own budget, his own corps of leaders, and his own flock. The lay character of Sunday school leadership may be responsible for an attitude still common among a number of clergymen, namely, that Christian nurture is of secondary significance within the ministry of the church.

EDUCATION PROGRAMS PROLIFERATE

During the first part of the nineteenth century, the Sunday school was virtually the only educational program in the churches. Toward the end of the century, two additional educational endeavors sprang into being. The first was the development of youth groups.

In 1881, Dr. Francis B. Clark formed a Young People's Society of Christian Endeavor in a Congregational church of which he was the pastor. The idea was taken up rapidly by other churches, and "Father Clark" became the founder of an interdenominational movement which spread across America and to other countries. Recognizing the value of this program, several denominations developed their own distinctive brand of young people's societies. It is of interest that both Sunday schools and youth societies began as interdenominational programs. Like the Sunday school, youth groups were a parallel organization rather than an integral part of the church.

The second educational development in the latter part of the nineteenth century was the formation of missionary societies. Some churches were antimissionary. Even Sunday schools refused to include missionary education in their curricula — it was their business to teach the Bible. Thus missionary-minded church members were forced to develop their own educational organizations. Women's missionary societies were formed that were both educational and promotional. Eventually there came into being a graded system of missionary societies, including programs for adolescent girls, separate organizations for adolescent boys, and clubs for junior, primary, and even kindergarten children.

EDUCATIONAL COMMITTEES ARE BORN

The proliferation of Christian education programs which began in the nineteenth century continued into the twentieth. The year 1901 saw the beginning of the vacation church school, or, as it was called then, the Daily Vacation Bible School. In 1918, another major educational development began — weekday religious education. A school principal in Gary, Indiana, became concerned because so many school children were receiving no religious instruction. He conceived a plan whereby the public school would release a period of school time each week during which the church could provide a program of religious education.

We have traced the development of several major educational programs — the Sunday school, youth societies, missionary education organizations, the daily vacation Bible school, and weekday religious education — but this is not the end of the list. There are many newer developments, such as resident and day camping, fellowship and encounter groups, church membership classes, graded schools of missions and evangelism, graded choirs, weekday clubs, and others.

In the early part of the twentieth century, some churches began to organize church-related committees of Christian education. In the church the need was obvious for some kind of leadership to provide overall planning and integration of its educational activities. Each independent program, with its own strong leaders, was competing with other programs and sometimes with the church for leadership, program time, budget, and personnel.

In addition to this practical reason for developing a committee or board, there was a theological reason.

There had been a growing understanding of the nature and mission of the church and of the responsibility for the teaching ministry belonging to the church as a whole. Therefore the church ought to determine and administer its teaching program through a group or committee elected by the church and responsible to the church.

THE COMMITTEE BECOMES A BOARD

A logical next step was to change the status of the committee on Christian education to that of a church board alongside the other major boards of the church. After all, this committee had responsibility for a major portion of the church's ministry; no church board had a more extensive program to administer. And there was a growing recognition of the significance of the teaching ministry.

During the years the board of Christian education has been functioning, its values increasingly have been appreciated: it makes the ministry of teaching an integral part of the church's ministry and program; it integrates the teaching program, thus avoiding overlapping and omissions; it enhances the importance of teaching in the minds of officers and teachers since they are officially appointed by the church through one of its major boards; it provides for continuity of policy and program; it can plan each part of the educational program in reference to the whole; it provides for democracy with authority; it provides a means for the continuous study of the educational program and the introduction of new methods and resources; and, in making policy decisions, it provides an opportunity for exchange of ideas.

	The Objective of the
Section 2	Church's Educational Ministry

THE OBJECTIVE is the end which we wish to achieve, the target toward which we aim, the ultimate goal of the entire educational process. It has several purposes:

1. The Objective provides a goal employed by the church to determine the form and content of its educational ministry.

2. The Objective provides an orientation for teachers which, while permitting flexibility to meet specific needs of pupils, gives an overall sense of direction and avoids purposeless activities and educational anarchy.

3. The Objective provides a framework within which an adequate evaluation of specific goals can be achieved.

Sixteen Protestant denominations, working together in the Cooperative Curriculum Project, adopted a statement upon which most Protestant groups have based their Objective. The following is an interpretation of one of these statements.[1]

[1] Design for Teaching-Learning, Prospectus II — 1970-71 (Valley Forge: American Baptist Board of Education and Publication), pp. 4-5.

AN INTERPRETATION

The objective of the church's educational ministry is

Every church must have a clear understanding of its objective in order to develop an effective educational ministry. It must face such questions as: What is the purpose of the educational ministry? What is to be accomplished?

that all persons

Our teaching ministry must not be limited to those who are presently within the Christian fellowship. There is no one anywhere who is not the object of God's concern. His kingdom has no barriers of culture, race, or caste. "Come with me and I will make you to become . . ." is Christ's call to every person.

be aware of God

God is more than a theory. He is active in the affairs of men. We confront him in the midst of life *now*. We approach him not as an idea to be understood but as a person to be known. It is our concern that all persons have a living, vital experience of God.

through his self-disclosure,

Our ultimate authority is God as he discloses himself in creation, in history, and supremely in Jesus Christ, his Son. The Bible records this revelation. It is inspired by the Holy Spirit and is the normative means through which the word of God comes to man.

especially his redeeming love as revealed in Jesus Christ,

Jesus is the central figure of our faith because he is the principal revealer of God's love. Through Christ, God takes action to save man from the destructiveness of his own sins. In the life, death, and resurrection of Jesus, God has broken the bondage of sin, released us from our captivity, and given us new life and hope.

and, enabled by the Holy Spirit,

The objective is trinitarian. It indicates the activity of *God*, the redemptive work of God in *Jesus Christ*, and the enabling, regenerating power of the *Holy Spirit*. Through the work of the Holy Spirit, God continues to confront man, judging his sin, calling him to repent, and offering a new life of freedom and wholeness.

respond in faith and love,

God takes the initiative in confronting man, but man must respond to God's gracious love and call. He must indicate that he desires the freedom and new life that God has won for him in Jesus Christ. When man refuses to respond, he perpetuates his lostness and tragic separation from God, and therefore from men.

that as new persons in Christ

There is need for a basic decision for Jesus Christ on the part of every person; therefore, conversion must be an essential concern of the teaching ministry. This is requisite to full discipleship and church membership. As "new persons in Christ," all Christians are called to be ministering servants who share a mutual responsibility to one another and to the world.

they may know who they are and what their human situation means,

"Who am I?" "Why am I here?" "Where am I going?" "Who is God?" "Who is my neighbor?" "What is the style of life which God intends?" "What does it mean to be a Christian presence in the world?" — These are some of the persistent life issues which demand a Christian response.

grow as sons of God

Life is not a meaningless maze; life has a purposeful plan. Our educational ministry is to help all persons "attain . . . to mature manhood, to the measure of the stature of the fulness of Christ" (Ephesians 4:13). To grow as sons of God is to open ourselves to receive the life-giving, energizing Spirit of God. Even though we respond in faith and love, we never fully attain the measure and stature of Jesus Christ. We remain redeemed sinners, looking forward to the coming age and to the fulfillment of life with God beyond death.

rooted in the Christian community,

To grow into Christian maturity, one must live within a community which can support and direct him. But not just any community will do. It must be guided and motivated by Jesus Christ. Only as one belongs to a supporting community of faith and love can he learn to participate effectively in the servant ministry of Christ. The entire life of the church is the mold within which Christian learning takes place.

live in obedience to the will of God in every relationship,

All life is sacred. "The earth is the Lord's and the fulness thereof, the world and those who dwell therein" (Psalm 24:1). Since all of life belongs to God, there are no areas or relationships exempt from his sovereign will. The faith of a Christian should be evidenced by his obedience to God in all of his relationships and actions.

fulfill their common vocation in the world,

"God . . . through Christ reconciled us to himself and gave us the ministry of reconciliation" (2 Corinthians 5:18). Our vocation in the world is reconciliation. God calls us to end hostility and estrangement wherever they exist. All men are called to this ministry, and the church must help them respond responsibly to their call. The structures of the church become not the end of our ministry, but the means. And the ultimate field is the world.

and abide in the Christian hope.

Man is restless and dissatisfied with much of his daily existence. In the midst of his anxieties, he longs for a relationship with that which is eternally meaningful. His hope lies in the assurance that God is the Lord of history and ultimately will triumph in and over it. The Christian faces the future in faith, believing that the last word in life will be God's. Christian hope gives new dimensions to experience. It helps one to move out of the welter of the past, through challenges of the present, into the glory of God's tomorrow.

Section 3 | The Teaching-Learning Encounter

MEMBERS of the board of Christian education should be vitally interested in all that happens to individuals in class and group situations from week to week. For this reason, much of the planning of the board will be directed towards the best possible use of curriculum resources so that all teaching-learning experiences are meaningful and relevant to the experience of each pupil.

Notice the hyphenated term "teaching-learning." This phrase emphasizes the fact that teaching is not all done by the teacher. The pupil must be an active participant in the experience, or else teaching simply will not come off. It is as futile to believe that teaching has happened when no one has learned as to think that someone has sold when no one has bought.

Let us get the feel of the teaching-learning encounter by examining some key words that are part of the vocabulary used by Christian educators today.

Communication is the foundation of teaching; there

is no teaching unless communication happens. Through communication, one is able to express his real meaning to another. While this is something that every teacher should be able to do, it is not an easy accomplishment. There are barriers to communication: the same words may convey diverse meanings to different people; what interests one person may have little appeal to another; anxieties and defenses get in the way. The teacher has a better chance to make meanings clear when he uses two-way rather than one-way communication. Misinterpretations and misunderstandings can be clarified. Feelings can be sensed. The teacher can discover where the pupil really is.

Dialogue is somewhat similar to communication. In his book *The Miracle of Dialogue*, Reuel Howe defines dialogue as "the serious address and response between two or more persons, in which the being and truth of each is confronted by the being and truth of the other."[1] Dialogue is seeing things eye to eye, a meeting of meanings. It is something more than conversation. It can take place even without the use of words. A good teacher will seek to engage the learners in dialogue regarding significant meanings.

Encounter is a word that suggests "againstness" or "collision." It is used in Christian education to mean a dialogue at a depth level involving real meanings and the whole person—thinking, feeling, and willing. Communication can take place at superficial levels; it can be casual and irrelevant. Encounter involves a stronger relationship, a meeting of eye to eye and heart to heart. When encounter occurs, the group takes on a dynamic quality, it comes alive, something meaningful is happening.

Meanings are the materials of dialogue and encounter. A meaning is an experience in the inner part of one's life, what he feels to be relevant to his deepest purposes and development. Victor Frankl has built an entire system of psychoanalysis around the significance of meaning. Whereas Freud emphasized the expression of sex as the basic quest underlying man's motivations and Karl Marx believed that the acquisition of material resources was the major motivating force in life, Frankl

[1] Reuel Howe, *The Miracle of Dialogue* (New York: The Seabury Press, Inc., 1963), p. 4.

stated that what man wants most is to have meaning. This is corroborated by Paul Tillich who believed that to be threatened by meaninglessness is one of man's greatest anxieties, along with his fear of death.

Members of the younger generation are rebelling against an educational system which they believe has limited meaning or value in the development of their personal lives or the life of the world. At least, we must agree with their basic premise, namely, that worthy education must have meaning which the learner regards as having value. Learning depends, then, upon the learner's judgment of "significance."

Experiential teaching has more value in the teaching-learning encounter than mere cognitive learning. For more than a hundred years, teaching was based upon an educational theory enunciated by Johann Friedrich Herbart, a German philosopher, who believed that

Knowledge determines the circle of thought,
And the circle of thought the character.

In other words, if we put the right information into people's minds, this will form some kind of matrix out of which good character will naturally emerge. In view of the findings of behaviorism, depth, and *Gestalt* psychologies, we can no longer accept the psychology upon which the Herbartian theory was based. We know that we must deal with whole persons, and not just their minds. We must take feelings into account, volitions, a person's life style, and his whole life situation. Teaching knowledge is not enough. A person may know what is right and good without its being true that he will do what is right and good. A person can know a whole encyclopedia of facts about God without having a vital experience of God in his life.

Action-reflection suggests two important ingredients in the teaching-learning encounter. The learner must be an active participant in the teaching-learning experience. There must be opportunity for him to initiate action, to explore, to discover, to experience. But he must also reflect upon his activity if it is to have a meaning. William James recognized this when he stated that we learn to skate in summer and swim in winter. He meant that we do not necessarily learn from experience, but from reflection upon the experience. Without reflection and evaluation, experience may be a bad teacher; it may teach us simply to go on doing the same thing over and over in the same way, even though it may be unworthy and meaningless.

Both action and reflection are important, and the action often must come first. We have the experience, and then learn the truth which it teaches. The great creeds of the church came this way: persons had vital religious experiences; then they attempted to formulate the meaning of the experiences in words. But the experience came first!

Internalize is a word borrowed from the social scientists. It means to appropriate truth at the deepest levels of one's being. It means much more than getting ideas. To internalize is to appropriate meanings until they enter the subconscious and become part of one's warp and woof, the very fabric of one's life. From the social scientists we also learn that one is more likely to internalize truth if he is a participant in the process, if he has a part in discovering it. Dialogue, then, is a better educational medium than monologue. The attitude, "Let us look for the answer to these questions together," is a better teaching stance than, "Here is the truth that I have discovered. Take it."

Self-disclosure is an important phrase in the statement of Objective in the preceding section, "that all persons be aware of God through his self-disclosure." Members of a previous generation would have used the word "revelation." It means the same thing: God reveals himself, discloses himself to man in a divine-human encounter. This does not refer to a revelation of information alone, but to a real and vital experience with God. The greatest record of God's self-disclosure is the Bible. In our study of the Bible, we learn how God disclosed himself to men of old, but we make a grievous mistake if we fail to understand that God's self-disclosure is still happening. God is not dead. He reveals himself as an active participant in the midst of our life today. Education that teaches only about what God did in the past is sterile unless it becomes a clue for discovering where God is working in the world today and how we may relate to him there.

Let us be assured that the classroom is not outside of God's precincts. Let the teacher be aware that when he goes to meet his class, God is there already, anxious to speak his word and disclose himself within the teaching-learning encounter.

The *world* is the arena in which the learners live, the place where they perform their ministry on behalf of Christ and his church. In the New Testament, the world is sometimes given an evil connotation, something to be avoided, or to overcome (James 1:27; John 16:33). But the world is considered also to be the object of God's love (John 3:16). Because God loved the world so much,

he sent his Son into the world that the world might be saved through him (John 3:17). And as Christ was sent into the world, so he sends his disciples into the world (John 17:18). This is the vocation of the Christian — to minister in the world. The church is the armory, but the world is the battleground.

Too often have we lived as if the church were an end in itself. Jesus did not say, "You are the light of the *church*." He said, "You are the light of the *world*." Jesus did not say, "Go into all the *church*," but "into all the *world*." Jesus did not say, "You shall be my witnesses in the *church*." He said that we should be his witnesses in the city (Jerusalem), in the ghetto (Samaria), in the suburbs (Judea), and the uttermost parts of the *world*. To be true to Jesus, the teaching ministry not only must provide nurture for personal growth, but also train persons for life and ministry in the world.

Love is a word with many meanings. Unfortunately, the English language has only one word to express them. The Greek language in which the New Testament was originally written had at least five, each one with distinctive nuances. The Greek word *agape* (a-gá-pe) expresses what Jesus meant when he said, "By this shall all men know that you are my disciples, that you have love one for another," or what Paul had in mind when he said "the greatest of these is love." *Agape*-love is the expression of a genuine concern for other persons, a desire to help the object of one's love rather than to possess and enjoy it for oneself. Increasingly, we recognize that everyone's greatest needs are to be loved and to love. The major requisite for teaching is the capacity for loving one's pupils.

Read again Paul's chapter on love in his first letter to the Corinthians, recognizing that originally the New Testament was written without chapter divisions. In other words, the thirteenth chapter is an integral part of the twelfth chapter, with no demarcation between them. In the twelfth chapter, Paul wrote about the relative importance of church leaders — apostles, prophets, teachers, and others. He concluded this discussion by saying that there is one role in the church which is more important than all the others: the ministry of loving. This is a requisite for anyone who wishes to serve as a leader in the church. The thirteenth chapter of First Corinthians is not a pretty, sentimental homily or essay on love; rather it describes the most important characteristic of a church leader — love. Whatever else a Christian teacher must do, the most important thing is that he shall love his pupils, and teach them to love.

Christian education is the teaching-learning encounter through which persons become "aware of God through his self-disclosure, especially his redeeming *love* as revealed in Jesus Christ, and, enabled by the Holy Spirit, respond in faith and *love*."

Section 4 | The Church's Ministry of Christian Education

THERE ARE four major settings in which education takes place: the family, the school, the community, and the church.

The family educates, although its influence is somewhat less than in past generations. The family has been discarding functions for many years. Services once provided by the home are now cared for by other agencies, and this has weakened family solidarity. Rapid changes in our society have created a generation gap. Today, many children are less willing to affirm their parents' scale of values or accept their authority. Still, the home is potentially and actually a significant educational institution. It is most influential in the development of preschool children. It can continue to be an effective educational medium throughout the school years if parents grow with their children and surround them with intelligent love.

The board of Christian education must surely be concerned about family life. The success of its own teaching endeavors will be conditioned by the support or lack of support provided by the home. The board will help parents, both by precept and example, to be good teachers of religion. It will seek to help every family to become a redemptive fellowship of persons who are committed to Christian goals.

The school educates. Since the days when education consisted of teaching only the three R's, schools have steadily grown in influence. In addition to traditional academic subjects, schools now provide training in vocational skills, the arts, and a large variety of extracurricular activities, and they frequently furnish services such as hot lunches, health checkups, dental care, vocational guidance, and personal counseling. In the mid-seventies, America will become the first nation in which a majority of its college-age youth will be attending a college or university. By 1980, virtually every youth in America will live within thirty miles of a college or university center. Also, the program of public education offerings for adults is expanding rapidly. In some states, the number of adults attending evening courses in schools and colleges almost equals the daytime enrollment of children and youth.

The board of Christian education will be interested in the schools of the community. It will support constructive programs for bettering school conditions. It will keep informed concerning school progress and encourage the election of competent persons to the school board.

The community exercises a powerful influence upon persons of all ages, and, since the advent of mass media, this influence has grown stronger. Newspapers, magazines, motion pictures, radio, and television bombard us with an array of facts and a conglomerate diversity of moral judgments. Persons are also greatly influenced by the mores and behavior patterns of their peer groups and the subcultures in the community to which they are related.

In the past, the board of Christian education has been concerned almost exclusively about the educational activities conducted within the four walls of the church and has ignored both the religious and ethical influences

of the community upon the learner, as well as the opportunities within the community for the expression of Christian witness and service as part of the board's educational program.

The board must recognize that much of the education of its constituents takes place outside the activities which it sponsors. In every community there are expressions of folk religion, that is, religious concepts that grow up spontaneously in the common life of the people. These folk religious concepts are often contradictory to the ethical demands of the Christian gospel ("You can't mix religion and business," "People living in poverty are lazy," "Members of the white race are ordained by God to enjoy a status of superiority," and others). Many church members are more greatly influenced by community mores than by the gospel. The board should recognize factors in the community that influence thinking and behavior patterns. A classroom discussion of the Christian interpretation of sexual behavior may have little motivational influence if in the same week pupils witness a pornographic movie at the community theater. Also, the self-interest of a political party may offset the church school's attempt to make Christ the Lord of political life. The church should help its constituents evaluate the community culture from a Christian perspective, and contribute to the development of community influences that are constructive and Christian. There are many positive as well as negative factors in community life — organizations serving personal and social needs, newspapers with constructive and forward-looking policies, books, magazines, and mass media programs that support Christian values. The community is a valid arena for the concern and action of the board.

The church teaches. As indicated in Section One, our nation developed an educational dichotomy in which the state accepts responsibility for "secular education" while to the church is given the responsibility for "religious education." The church exercises its teaching responsibility in three ways. First, the church teaches through the quality of its corporate life: the love that members express for one another; the demonstration and concern by church members and groups for those outside the church fellowship; the values that it considers important, exemplified by its programmed activities and its budget. Second, the church teaches through the ministry of its members as they live in the world. As nonchurch members hear church members witnessing to their faith and observe Christian characteristics in their manner of living, they are learning something about the church and hopefully something about the gospel as well. Third, the church teaches through a program of planned activities — classes, encounter groups, workshops, camps, conferences, etc., by which it endeavors to achieve its objective.

STRUCTURED TEACHING PROGRAMS

To provide an effective teaching ministry, churches must design educational programs which offer a reasonable expectation that the church will be able to communicate the gospel and prepare persons for their Christian vocation in the world. Various structured programs have been developed for this purpose. Let us examine the characteristics of those most commonly employed.

THE CHURCH SCHOOL

For many churches, the church school is the basic teaching-learning opportunity. It is a school for all persons. It includes both those who have responded to the call of Christ and those who are inquiring into the meaning of the Christian gospel. Classes for learners meet at a designated time once a week. Traditionally the church school has been held on Sundays, but some churches are experimenting with classes held on weekdays, either after school or on Saturday mornings. Church school classes usually meet in the church building, but may meet in other locations, such as homes, business buildings, or retreat centers.

An essential in any learning group is that there be sufficient time for communication and the development of interpersonal relations. This calls for a maximum of prime, uninterrupted teaching time. When children have the benefit of an expanded session, the entire program for children may continue for two or two and a half hours.

The administration of the church school is the responsibility of the board of Christian education, working in close cooperation with the general superintendent. All church school leadership will operate within the policies of the board.

THE EVENING FELLOWSHIP

As indicated in Section One, the idea of a training program for young people meeting on Sunday evenings developed in the latter part of the nineteenth century. Of recent origin is the addition of other age-group programs, particularly for adult groups meeting simultaneously with youth meetings. Sometimes persons of all age groups combine for a joint or family worship program in addition to the age-group sessions. In some churches, groups meet at different times — the youth meeting on Sunday evenings or on week nights, the children meeting on Sunday afternoons or on weekdays after school, and the adults meeting on a week night or on Sunday.

The purposes of evening fellowship groups are: (1) to meet the need for a new depth of fellowship; (2) to provide additional opportunities for experiencing the redemptive activity of the Holy Spirit within face-to-face groups; (3) to provide spiritual enrichment for each person, each family unit, and the church as a whole; (4) to train persons for responsible church membership and leadership; (5) to provide an arena for open discussion of relevant issues; (6) to enable church members to witness as Christians in the life and work of the world.

There are many who feel that the traditional time allowed for evening groups — fifty or sixty minutes — does not permit encounter in depth. Some groups meet for two hours.

THROUGH-THE-WEEK EDUCATION

The term *weekday religious education* connotes a type of religious instruction that takes place one hour a week on time released by the public school. The unique contribution of this educational setting is to help children and youth look at school experiences and learnings from the perspective of Christian faith. Much that is encountered in school, whether in classroom instruction or in school relationships and activities, has a bearing on who we think man is, what the function of society is, and what the meaning and purpose of human existence is. The church has a responsibility to witness to the profound convictions of the Christian faith regarding such matters.

Weekday programs on released time are usually conducted interdenominationally through a local council of churches, a ministerial association, or a special organization created for this purpose. Many school systems require interdenominational sponsorship. Weekday schools operate in such close contact with public education that it is paramount that the weekday school represent a quality of teaching which compares favorably with public school experience, or children get the impression that religious learning is less important than secular education.

Released-time education is not the only kind of "through-the-week" education available to the church. Many churches conduct classes and projects after school hours or on Saturdays.

CAMPING

The program of camps and summer conferences is one of the significant developments of our generation. Here a new dimension of Christian living begins to emerge for children, youth, and adults — a fuller understanding of self, a new sense of responsibility, a better relationship with others, and a vital, living relationship with God.

Since the camp program is usually a joint venture with regional, state, or city denominational organizations, the board of Christian education may take the following steps: (1) recognize the camping program as an integral part of the local church's educational ministry; (2) recruit campers and conferees on the basis of their particular needs and the programs that will best fulfill these needs; (3) provide a share of the leadership, as requested by the sponsoring organization; (4) encourage the church to support the camping program with special gifts; (5) arrange for "camperships" through which the church pays part of each camper's expenses.

Many churches conduct a program of day camping for one or more weeks during the summer, or on one or two days a week for several weeks. Available camping sites or public parks within commuting distance are normally used. A day camp is not just a Sunday school held out of doors. Day camping can have real worth if leaders are sensitive to the values of camping activities and trained in the use of camping techniques.

VACATION CHURCH SCHOOL

The vacation church school is a program conducted for approximately two and a half hours five mornings a week for a period of two or three weeks during the summer. Some variations include programs held in the evenings, or on one or two days a week for a period of weeks. The vacation church school has distinctive advantages: it provides unhurried time for learning experiences; it has daily continuity, no week-long intervals for forgetting; it makes possible the development of morale and "groupness"; it allows for creative experiences; it is a valuable contact agency for discovering and recruiting unreached children and entire families; it provides a constructive use of summertime leisure.

The vacation church school may be conducted by a single church or by a grouping of churches which share facilities and leadership resources.

ENCOUNTER GROUPS

The proliferation of small, face-to-face encounter groups is one of the most significant contemporary developments in the life of the church. Such groups may meet in the church building or in the homes of group members. They are informal in character and evoke the active participation of group members in discussion and leadership. Usually they are limited to a total of twelve or fourteen persons. Members accept the discipline of regular attendance and required reading. Encounter groups may be developed for purposes of study, worship, personal growth, social action, or a combination of these. The groups have made significant contributions to the renewal of individuals and of entire churches.

SHORT-TERM GROUPS FOR SPECIAL PURPOSES

Short-term groups are scheduled to meet on Sunday evenings, on week nights, or at other times that fit the convenience of their members. Such groups are conducted for a limited time — four to twelve sessions — and for a particular purpose, such as a school of missions, a school of Christian stewardship, a church membership class, a parent-education class, a church-in-world conference, a leader development course, or other special groups. Some denominations promote graded schools of missions with classes for all age groups above the kindergarten.

RETREATS

One-day or weekend retreats are growing in usage and significance. They may help persons reach deeper levels of insight regarding themselves and their relationship with God and with others. They may serve the purpose of furthering an understanding of the mission of the church, or making a new commitment to God's purposes, or serving more effectively in the world. They may be used for church planning or for leader development. The retreat provides an admirable setting for the development of group morale and team building.

FAMILY LIFE EDUCATION

The church can help the home at the point of special needs. It can provide resources for worship in the home, furnish assistance in the sex education of children and youth, help parents to understand the needs of their children at different stages of development, show concern for shut-ins, help to bridge the generation gap, and enable parents to adjust to changing life situations, such as entering the "empty nest" stage or approaching the experiences of retirement.

Churches are paying special attention to the needs of one-person families, who previously have been ignored. This constitutes a surprising number of persons.

INTERDENOMINATIONAL PROGRAMS

There is a developing trend to carry on selected educational programs in cooperation with other churches. As has been suggested, weekday religious education on public school released time is usually conducted interdenominationally, and must be. Jointly sponsored vacation church schools, youth fellowship groups, and programs of leader development are common. In a growing number of cases, both Protestant and Roman Catholic groups are participating in ecumenical educational projects. Such programs give groups a chance to clarify and demonstrate common goals by understanding their differences.

In developing cooperative programs, representatives of the board of Christian education, or persons selected by the board, are the logical individuals to serve on interdenominational sponsoring committees. Churches should be willing to work cooperatively whenever it is apparent that better results can be attained through cooperative efforts.

GUIDELINES FOR DETERMINING PROGRAM ACTIVITIES

The preceding pages make it clear that the church has access to a plethora of program structures and designs. The problem faced by most boards is not a dearth of program possibilities, but rather the necessity of limiting the programs in order to utilize effectively the potential of their human resources — available leadership and the participation capacity of their constituents. Although a board should be thoroughly familiar with available program structures, it should limit its activities to those which can meet the most significant needs.

The board should have two kinds of need in mind.

First, there is the need for a basic program of Christian nurture. This basic program should provide an understanding of the biblical revelation and develop a growing relationship of the learners with God and his purposes. It should be the major program through which the church seeks to accomplish its educational objective. In most churches, this is attempted through the church school which usually meets on Sunday mornings.

In the basic program, a sequence of experiences is planned in such a way that each stage of development takes the learner further along toward the realization of the Objective. Each person is fitted into the group that will make possible his maximum growth.

Second, churches should develop additional educational activities to supplement their basic program. For example, a church may develop a number of small encounter groups of youth and/or adults to meet personal needs of their members, or to train them for significant ministry in the community. Or a church may plan a program of summer activities for children in recognition of their leisure time and the need for constructive summer activities. Or a church near a college campus may develop a special ministry to and with college students and faculty members. Or a church may plan a class for new members, recognizing the need for authentic church membership and informed and dedicated church members.

Here are some factors to be taken into account when developing the educational ministry of the church:
• Providing a basic program of Christian nurture that is effective at all age levels
• Identifying crucial personal needs and organizing educational programs that will meet them
• Recognizing pressing needs in the community and discovering ways the educational program can contribute to their solution
• Evaluating the current educational program and strengthening weak elements

• Starting new groups to meet important unmet needs
• Developing a statement of priorities, recognizing that the board cannot create all the programs it would like
• Eliminating programs that have the least potential meaning

Starting new groups is far easier than eliminating old ones that are nonproductive. Loyalty to an established group is sometimes stronger than commitment to ministry. Barren branches that sap nutriment from the life of the tree but bear no fruit are a luxury that the church cannot afford. Either they should be cut off or grafted with new life and productivity. To excise an ineffective group is always painful and sometimes disastrous. It must be done with loving care. This can be facilitated if members of the group have a strong sense of the church's mission and are represented adequately in the planning and decision-making process.

Because of the hazards in terminating unproductive groups, there is a trend toward starting new groups that have very specific purposes and a built-in terminal date when the group is to be evaluated in terms of its achievement, and then either continued or terminated. Ad hoc groups with specific goals and termination dates are becoming more popular.

Section 5 | Functions of the Board

THE BOARD of Christian education, we can assume, has responsibility for the total teaching ministry of the church, but this assumption creates some practical problems. The teaching ministry is only one of several ministries in the church: proclamation, worship, fellowship, witness, and service. As part of a whole ministry, these separate ministries are interrelated and often overlap. For example, not one of these other ministries can be achieved without making some use of teaching procedures. Sometimes determining the boundary line between the function of the board of Christian education and the work of other boards and committees is difficult. The following distinction will be helpful:

1. There are some functions which clearly belong to the teaching ministry, such as the work of the church school, the youth fellowship, the vacation church school, and through-the-week education. These programs focus upon the development of the individual.

2. There are functions in which teaching plays a subordinate role to the work of other boards. The worship life of the church, visitation evangelism, and conduct of service ministries in the community belong to this category. These functions will be the responsibility of other boards or specially appointed task groups. In such cases, the board of Christian education may be called upon to provide assistance.

This section will deal only with the first category — tasks which are clearly within the scope of the board of Christian education and for which it has the major responsibility.

In general, the board of Christian education formulates the policies of the church's educational ministry and sees that these policies are implemented effectively. This function may be delineated more specifically in terms of the following responsibilities:

STUDY

The board needs to carry on a continuous study of its work. Areas for investigation will include biblical theology, the philosophy and program of Christian education, and the needs of the world which must be met through the teaching ministry. Such a study may be conducted in several ways: (1) time in each meeting of the board may be used for serious study and discussion; (2) a day or preferably a weekend retreat can be used for a concentrated study in a particular area; (3) members of the board may do individual reading based upon a systematic plan and make summary reports to the board for its enrichment and discussion.

ESTABLISH AND INTERPRET THE OBJECTIVE

If there is one thing that is more important than any other, it is that members of the board have a clear understanding of its purpose. They must share common assumptions about the nature of the church and the educational ministry.

Section Two presented a brief interpretation of a statement of the Objective. Here is a good place to begin. Let the board make a thorough study of this statement and then adopt it as the board's Objective, either as it stands or with modifications growing out of the study.

It is not enough for board members to know and

use the Objective — it should be studied as well by all teaching personnel so they have a clear concept of the purpose of their teaching. At each age-group level, teachers should ask, "How does this Objective apply to the pupils in my group?"

Since teaching is the ministry and responsibility of the entire church, the entire membership should know about and understand the Objective of the Educational Ministry. To interpret the Objective to the teaching staff and the constituency is a responsibility of the board and the pastor.

DISCOVER NEEDS

The discovery of needs should be a continuous process, an ongoing "order of the day," but a more systematic checkup should be made annually just before the program for a new year is planned. Two kinds of needs can be examined.

First, there are internal needs, weaknesses within the present program which should be strengthened, such as an adult class which would benefit by greater participation of its members, or a youth group which ought to be challenged by a better program. Or there may be vacuums that should be filled — developing a middle high class in the church school, or planning more adult encounter groups, or providing for a program of visitation for parents of nursery children.

Second, there are external needs in the life of the local community, or of the larger community — the world — to which the teaching ministry can make a contribution. For example, are there persons confined to their homes who have real needs that no one is meeting? Are there children in need of tutoring in order to avoid becoming school dropouts? Are there ways in which suburbanites can relate to needs in the inner city? Are there young people who need counseling concerning the draft? Are there working mothers who need the facilities of a day nursery? Can the educational ministry play a part in solving these problems? How? Underlying this question is the assumption that the educational program should educate for mission as well as for nurture.

Before addressing itself to the discussion of needs, the board can facilitate the process by appointing a small task force to gather data and make a preliminary investigation. To accomplish its purpose, the task force may send a data collector to all teaching personnel and members of church boards. The data collector can be quite simple — just several open-end statements:

1. The weaknesses in our educational program are. . . .
2. The vacuums in our educational program are. . . .
3. Some of the most important needs of the community (outside the church) that must be met are. . . .
4. The educational program of our church could help to meet these needs by. . . .

After the task group has gathered the data, it should present a summary report to the board for discussion and action.

DETERMINE THE PROGRAM

Planning a program to achieve the Objective is a long-term, comprehensive process. It requires study, analysis, continual evaluation, consultation with Christian education workers, and continual updating in the light of new trends and insights.

During the past century and a half, the church has developed numerous structures and programs to meet emerging needs in the teaching ministry. Some of these are listed in the section preceding this. Every board should become acquainted with available programs and resources and employ those that can be used effectively in meeting the needs of its particular situation.

SELECT CURRICULUM RESOURCES

The choice of a curriculum design and supporting resources is clearly the responsibility of the board. To permit each department superintendent or teacher to select whatever curriculum resources he may wish to use results inevitably in a chaotic hodgepodge. Imagine a public school without a systematic overall design, in which each teacher could decide what courses would be taught and what textbooks would be used.

In choosing a curriculum plan and resources, every church should consider the values which derive from using its own denominational program:

• The denominational curriculum plan and resources are the product of many competent persons — scholars, editors, field workers, and writers — who have dedicated their lives to the ministry of Christian teaching.

• The curriculum design has a unified philosophy and a consistent theological orientation.

• Materials are field-tested by a random sample of churches in the denomination and evaluated by a grass-roots reaction of pastors and other church leaders.

• The denominational program of leader development, including conferences, demonstration-observation days, workshops and laboratory schools, provides training related to the denominational curriculum plan.

SELECT, RECRUIT, AND DEVELOP LEADERS

If there is a church-wide committee on personnel, the board will work closely with that committee. If there is no such church committee, the board will take the entire responsibility, working through its own Chairman or Committee on Leader Development.

When a person is needed to fill a particular position, consideration should be given to everyone seeming to possess the necessary qualifications. When the selection has been made, the board should officially ratify the choice and arrange for one or preferably two persons to interview the prospective leader. One member of the team may well represent the specific department or program unit in which the person is to work — a lead teacher or the department superintendent. The second team member may represent the church at large — the pastor, the general superintendent, or the chairman of the board. During the course of the interview, the visitors will give a clear picture of the position and its importance, exhibit and describe briefly the curriculum resources to be used, indicate what training is available to support the leader, and show how the position in question is related significantly to the mission of the church.

In addition to selecting and recruiting leaders, the board is responsible for providing them with meaningful training opportunities. Perhaps this is the board's most important role. Section Nine is devoted to this function (p. 31).

PREPARE AND ADMINISTER THE EDUCATIONAL BUDGET

Since teaching is a major ministry of the church, the expenses of the entire teaching program should be financed by the church budget. There are still some church schools with a separate, independent treasury, but this is one of the vestigial remains from the era when the Sunday school was a separate and parallel organization. The church school should not be expected to pay all its expenses out of its own receipts from the pupils. If there is an offering in the church school, the money so received should go into the church treasury, and the church should pay all church school expenses.

The board of Christian education should prepare annually an "asking budget" which would include all the projects and programs the board plans to sponsor during the new fiscal year. In drawing up the budget, the board should indicate two sets of figures, one showing the minimum requirements for the program; the other, desirable additional funds. After the budget committee of the church has prepared a total church budget, taking all interests into account, and has adjusted the budget in the light of church pledging, a realistic budget will be adopted by the church, which then will provide the board with its working budget for the new year.

Giving to the denomination's world mission should be an integral part of the educational program, regardless of how the church school offering is administered. A definite portion of each week's offering should be designated for this purpose. This can be done either through the use of duplex envelopes in the church school, or through the designation of a specific percent of the offering, in which case the students should clearly understand that this portion of their offering is helping to undergird the world mission.

SAMPLE ASKING BUDGET

	Minimum	Desirable
The Church School	$_____	$_____
Includes curriculum resources and administrative expense		
The Evening Fellowship	_____	_____
Program expense		
Vacation Church School	_____	_____
Program expense		
School of Missions	_____	_____
Through-the-Week Education	_____	_____
(Itemize activities)		
Christian Family Life Education	_____	_____
Resources for seasonal observance in the home.		
Outdoor Education	_____	_____
(Itemize projects)		
Ministry with Children	_____	_____
Ministry with Youth	_____	_____
Ministry with Adults	_____	_____
New Equipment	_____	_____
Multimedia Resources	_____	_____
Library	_____	_____
Leader Development	_____	_____
Includes scholarships for laboratory schools, cost of leadership classes, camperships, etc.		
Special Programs	_____	_____
Such as a recognition dinner for church school staff.		
Board Expenses—administrative	_____	_____
Miscellaneous	_____	_____
Total		
	$_____	$_____

ALLOCATE SPACE AND PROVIDE EQUIPMENT

The board of Christian education should proceed on the assumption that a church building belongs to the whole church and that the church should decide how its building is to be used. Unfortunately, churches do not always operate upon this basis. Organized adult classes and other church groups sometimes act as though they own the space in which they meet, perhaps because they were helpful in raising funds to finance the building when it was built, or have provided the furnishings.

If the church building is to be used in ways that best further its ministry, flexibility is needed so that the space can be redistributed from time to time to meet changing conditions. The attendance in one adult class may have shrunk through the years, and it may no longer need the large room it occupies. The kindergarten may be occupying a smaller room and pushing the walls out because of its growth. Perhaps these two groups should exchange rooms, thus providing ample space for the burgeoning kindergarten while still giving the adult class enough space to meet its needs.

Every church should have an annual "moving day" when each class and department moves out of its room, at least psychologically, and then returns to quarters assigned by the board. This should not imply a drastic change in any one year, but it does permit necessary adjustments. The philosophy of this plan should be interpreted carefully in advance so that groups will feel a minimum of resentment about the changes that need to be made.

Periodically, the board should conduct a survey of all equipment, including room decorations and furnishings, discard items that are obsolete or unneeded, replace or repair articles that are broken or decrepit, and see that the educational rooms are attractive and clean. Major alterations or redecoration should be planned for the period of the year when church school attendance is lowest.

When new buildings are constructed, the building committee of the church should consult with the board concerning specifications for educational rooms. Also the board may seek professional architectural counsel through its city, state, or regional director of Christian education.

COORDINATE CHRISTIAN EDUCATION ACTIVITIES

A calendar of schedules, meetings, and activities of all phases of the educational program ought to be developed by the board in order to avoid overlapping and competition. All activities and projects of the various groups, including the committees of the board, should be interrelated so that they support each other as parts of an overall church program.

The educational program needs to be correlated not only internally, but also with the total program of the church through an advisory council or church board in which the board of Christian education is represented along with others.

Another relationship that demands correlation is with community programs, such as cooperative through-the-week education projects, vacation church schools, leader-ship development schools, and also nonecclesiastical programs, such as school activities which would compete with church-sponsored projects.

PLAN FOR SPECIAL DAYS

Every church faces the problems arising from the observance of special days or seasons throughout the year. Someone has to decide which of these special days will be observed in the educational program and in what manner. Logically, this should be done by the board of Christian education as a whole. How will each holiday be observed —by the entire church, by the total church school, or at the discretion of each department? Is there a value in having the whole church family gather for some celebrations, such as Children's Day, Christmas, New Year's Day? How can the board assist families in celebrating special days in the home?

EVALUATE

To have significance, evaluation must be done with care and insight. It should be based upon something more than pooling everybody's opinions. Some objective standards of measurement should be utilized. Evaluation should not be limited to quantitative measurements of growth, but should include the kind of meaning which Paul attached to building up the body of Christ (Ephesians 4:11-16). This function is so important that Section Twelve is devoted to "Evaluating the Church's Educational Ministry."

EXTEND THE TEACHING MINISTRY

The church has a responsibility for extending the ministry of teaching to those who are not now being reached by existing programs. The world God loves includes those whose lives the church touches lightly or not at all. Some of these persons live in proximity to

---

FUNCTIONS OF THE BOARD
Study
Establish and Interpret the Objective
Discover Needs
Determine the Program
Select Curriculum Resources
Select, Recruit, and Develop Leaders
Prepare and Administer the Educational Budget
Allocate Space and Provide Equipment
Coordinate Christian Education Activities
Plan for Special Days
Evaluate
Extend the Teaching Ministry
Develop an Educational Consciousness

the church building and could be enrolled in existing educational programs if specific efforts were made to find and recruit them. Psychological barriers may demand the establishment of an outpost teaching program, perhaps in a home or a storefront meeting place. A systematic census or a "Winning the Children for Christ" story hour may be helpful. The church has to be far more creative and imaginative than it has been in the past if it wants to be heard in today's world. Some churches are using the friendly setting of a coffee hour, a child care center for working mothers, or tutoring of dropouts as outreach ministries. These may not be suitable projects in your church and community, but this is a time for risking and daring, and from every experience, whether it succeeds or fails, we derive valuable learning. The outreach of the church should be a vital concern of the board.

Develop an Educational Consciousness

The board of Christian education can interpret to the entire congregation the significance, purposes, and plans of the teaching program, helping them to recognize the importance of teaching in the ministry of the church and the responsibility for every church member to be a growing person, a learner. Possible methods include items in church bulletins, articles in papers (both church and community), posters on bulletin boards, exhibits of projects and articles developed in the teaching program, an evening "open house" for parents, parent-teacher meetings, Children's Day and other special day observances, and the presentation of color slides, amateur movies, or snapshots taken by individual members depicting the church's teaching ministry at work. The annual report to the church can also be helpful, if it can be done in more than a perfunctory manner.

Section 6 | Structuring the Board

Five models for structuring the administration of Christian education in the local church are outlined in this section. The first four models relate specifically to the board of Christian education. The fifth model refers to a single-church-board operation.

The first four models are not mutually exclusive, but their features can be combined. In fact, basic Model A should be included in Models B, C, and D. Model C should include all the features of Models A and B.

Model A.   A Basic Plan

The board of Christian education should include from three to twelve elected members, depending upon the size of the church. The following is suggested for consideration:

Under 100 members	3 members
100 to 500 members	6 members
500 to 1,000 members	9 members
Over 1,000 members	12 members

Members should be elected for a three-year term, with the stipulation that they will not succeed themselves in office after serving one, or at the most, two terms, without one year intervening. In addition to the elected members, there are several persons who should serve by virtue of their office as ex officio members with voting privileges. They are: the general superintendent of the church school, the pastor, and the director/

minister of Christian education. The board should choose a chairman and a secretary from among the elected members.

Some suggested responsibilities for the officers and ex officio members are listed.

The General Chairman

1. Serves as general administrator of the total educational program.

2. Helps the board organize, arranges for and conducts meetings.

3. Prepares a tentative agenda for each meeting, having in mind the basic Objective, the program goals of the board, and the specialized interests of each board member.

4. Helps the board make assignments to members in keeping with basic policies, and checks to see that all assignments are fulfilled.

5. Helps the board prepare and supervise the budget.

6. Prepares or authorizes reports to the church and denominational agencies.

7. Serves as ex officio member of all committees of the board.

8. Represents the board on the church advisory council.

9. Counsels with the pastoral ministers concerning the educational program.

THE SECRETARY

1. Keeps accurate minutes of meetings.

2. Provides members with copies of minutes as soon as possible after each meeting.

3. Helps implement and coordinate a system of records for the educational program.

4. Makes available to the board and other educational personnel significant data gathered from the records.

5. Mails meeting notices to members well in advance of meetings.

THE PASTOR

1. Counsels and gives leadership in planning and implementing the church's educational ministry.

2. Helps correlate the educational program with the activities of other groups in the church.

3. Assists in finding and recruiting potential leaders in the educational ministry.

4. Serves as "teacher of teachers," sharing this role with the director/minister of Christian education.

5. Gives leadership to specific church-wide educational goals and projects.

6. Helps the church do long-range planning on the basis of needs in the church and community.

7. Interprets to the church the educational Objective and the annual perspective and program.

8. Counsels teachers with special needs and problems.

THE MINISTER, OR DIRECTOR, OF CHRISTIAN EDUCATION

When a church has a director/minister of Christian education, he will carry out most of the responsibilities indicated above for the pastor. Nevertheless, the pastor, as administrator of the entire ministry of the church, should continue his relationship with the board, or the ministry of the church will suffer from fragmentation. The pastor will counsel with the director/minister in regular staff sessions, and support him and his policies in board meetings. The director/minister of Christian education will be in constant communication with the senior minister and other staff persons interpreting decisions and policies, and sharing his own personal concerns for the teaching ministry.

THE GENERAL CHURCH SCHOOL SUPERINTENDENT

1. Helps the board determine policies for the church school and administers these policies.

2. Seeks to maintain an effective church school organization.

3. Sees that such mechanical features as taking the roll and the offering, checking on absentees, contacting prospective pupils, and assigning new students to proper groups are cared for efficiently and with a minimum of distraction.

4. Cooperates with the board in implementing an adequate plan for providing substitute teachers.

5. Cooperates with the board in providing training opportunities for church school leaders.

MODEL B. A BOARD WITH ASSIGNED RESPONSIBILITIES

Model B recommends that every elected member be assigned a specific responsibility. In a board with six elected members, these may be: (1) general chairman; (2) chairman of ministry with children; (3) chairman of ministry with youth; (4) chairman of ministry with adults; (5) chairman of leader development; (6) chairman of education for missions. In this plan, anyone other than the general chairman may be asked to serve as secretary.

There are several reasons for assigning specific responsibilities to each member. First, each person can work to become a specialist in his particular area. Second, this model provides a balance on the board with each important phase of work represented. Third, through the chairmen of ministry with children, youth, and adults, it is possible to maintain a healthy two-way communication between the board and departmental leadership in the church school. Fourth, many questions

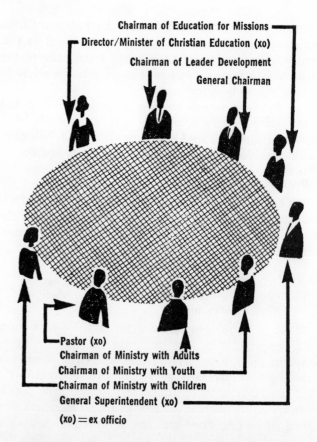

Chairman of Education for Missions
Director/Minister of Christian Education (xo)
Chairman of Leader Development
General Chairman

Pastor (xo)
Chairman of Ministry with Adults
Chairman of Ministry with Youth
Chairman of Ministry with Children
General Superintendent (xo)

(xo) = ex officio

Board of Christian Education (medium-sized church)

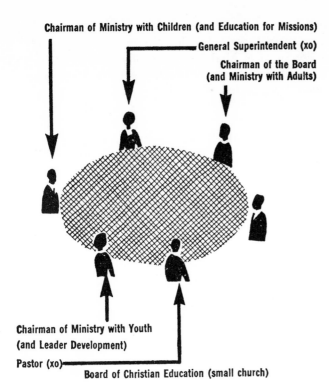

Chairman of Ministry with Children (and Education for Missions)

General Superintendent (xo)

Chairman of the Board
(and Ministry with Adults)

Chairman of Ministry with Youth
(and Leader Development)

Pastor (xo)

Board of Christian Education (small church)

of a specialized nature can be referred to individual board members and their committees for consideration and thus save valuable time of the board as a whole. Fifth, by having a particular function for which he feels responsible, every board member will serve more faithfully and effectively.

The small church may prefer a board of only three elected members, in which case a doubling up of responsibilities may be advisable. As a "for instance," the responsibility of leader development may be assigned to the chairman of ministry with children, education for missions may be assigned to the chairman of ministry with youth, and the chairman of ministry with adults may be asked to serve as general chairman. Several combinations of functions may be feasible, except that two age-group functions, such as chairman of ministry with children and chairman of ministry with youth, should not be assigned to the same person.

CHAIRMAN OF MINISTRY WITH CHILDREN
CHAIRMAN OF MINISTRY WITH YOUTH
CHAIRMAN OF MINISTRY WITH ADULTS

These age-group chairmen are chosen because of their competence in their respective fields. They understand the age group for whom they have responsibility. They are acquainted with good educational procedures that are relevant to their respective age groups. They have a good relationship with department superintendents and lead teachers in the church school and with other age-group leaders. They should be related to the process of selecting and training leaders for their age-group divisions. They should be capable of supervising the teaching in their respective departments and providing counseling assistance. Material in Section Seven will be particularly helpful to these three chairmen.

CHAIRMAN OF LEADER DEVELOPMENT

1. Helps the board plan for the development and training of all educational leaders.

2. Administers or arranges for the administration of leadership classes, schools, workshops, seminars, etc.

3. Supervises the recruitment of persons for camps, conferences, and laboratory schools.

4. Cooperates with age-group chairmen to secure needed resource books and multimedia equipment and resources.

5. May cooperate with age-group chairmen in providing supervisory services.

CHAIRMAN OF EDUCATION FOR MISSIONS

1. Helps the board develop outreach programs to discover and contact the unreached.

2. Understands and interprets community needs so that the board can plan an educational program that is relevant to the local situation.

3. Helps the church develop an effective program of missionary education and use approved annual missionary education resources.

4. Promotes stewardship education in the church.

5. Promotes education for social concern and action.

6. May serve as a member of the church committee on Christian social concern.

OTHER ASSIGNED RESPONSIBILITIES

Larger churches may have boards of nine or even twelve elected members, in which case the additional persons should be assigned other specific responsibilities. Here are some possibilities.

The person serving as *secretary* can be freed of other responsibilities.

A *Chairman of Family Life* can help further the interests of the Christian family. He can help the church conduct family emphasis programs that will serve to compensate for the church's tendency to fracture the family by structures that divide persons by ages and sex. He can help in the promotion of Christian Family Week and other family observances. He can foster reading and devotional life in the home. He can work with age-group chairmen in providing adequate programs of sex education and preparation for marriage. If qualified, he can assist the pastor in the counseling of families with marital problems.

A *Chairman of the Church Arts* can help foster the church's use of music, art, and drama. If the church has a graded program of choirs, he can work with the music leadership to see that good educational techniques are used with youth and children's choirs and that the choir program is integrated with other educational activities. He can develop competence in the field of religious art and serve the entire educational program as a resource in this area. He can give leadership in the field of religious drama, providing or securing dramatic leadership to produce religious dramas, supervise the church's dramatic wardrobe and other dramatic effects. He can publicize arts programs in the community that can make a contribution to Christian understanding and appreciation.

A *co-chairman* can be assigned to work with each of the age-group chairmen. This has the added value of providing continuity of program when the chairman of an age group can no longer serve.

MODEL C. A BOARD WITH ASSIGNED RESPONSIBILITIES AND COMMITTEES

This plan assumes the operation of a board with assigned responsibilities, as outlined under Model B. In addition, functioning of chairmen, particularly the age-group chairmen, with and through committees is suggested.

Age-group committees should include departmental superintendents or lead teachers with the possible addition of one or two parents and someone related to public education. Thus the committee on ministry with children would include the superintendents of the nursery, kindergarten, primary, middler, and junior departments, plus the parent of a preschool child, the parent of a child in the elementary grades, and an elementary grade public school teacher. The committee on ministry with youth may include department superintendents or lead teachers in the junior high, middle high, and senior high departments, plus youth representing each fellowship group, one or two parents, and a high school teacher. The committee on ministry with adults may include a representative from each adult class in the church school and each adult group in the church.

Age-group committees will consider such matters as the age-group program, curriculum resources, personnel, leader development, evaluation, administrative problems, and plans for special days. Quarterly meetings should be sufficient. They provide a valuable liaison between the board of Christian education and the work of the various program units. Age-group committees are an instrument for initiating plans. They can greatly facilitate the work of the board and save valuable board meeting time by bringing well-considered recommendations to the board for approval.

Some boards may wish to establish other committees, such as a committee on leader development, or a committee on education for missions. Others may prefer to function in these areas through the use of task groups as described in Model D. If a committee is established, persons who represent important phases of the program should be included. A committee on leader development should have members representing the three age groups, preferably the chairmen of ministry with children, with youth, with adults. A committee on education for missions should include persons who represent this interest in other groups, such as the youth groups and the men's and women's organizations.

MODEL D. A BOARD OPERATING WITH TASK GROUPS

A task group is an ad hoc committee with a limited tenure. In other words, it is a task force appointed to accomplish a particular job within a given length of time. Some boards carry on their program entirely through task groups, or with a combination of permanent committees and task groups. In using the task group concept, the following guidelines may be helpful.

1. The task must be important, meaningful in its relationship to the objective, and relevant to current needs and priorities.

2. The task to be performed must be clearly described and understood.

3. The time within which the task is to be accomplished should be specified.

4. The number of persons appointed to serve as the task group should be commensurate with the demands of the task — too few may not get the job done and too many will be a waste of manpower.

5. The task group should be composed of persons who have the kind of ability that the task requires.

6. At its conclusion, the task should be evaluated. In some cases, intermediate checkpoints should be included in the task description.

7. If not finished at its completion date, the task can be continued for an extended period, or assigned to another group for completion, or discontinued.

8. When a task is completed, the task group should be disbanded.

MODEL E. THE CHURCH WITH A SINGLE BOARD

Traditional structures of the free churches include several boards (deacons, trustees, Christian education) which meet monthly and whose programs are correlated through a church council. However, some churches prefer to function through a single church board which represents within itself all phases of the church's ministry. Such a plan has some peculiar values: it insures correlation of all programs and makes it possible to plan in terms of the total ministry of the church. Such a plan may have particular merit for use in the small church with limited leadership resources.

Each church must work out the membership of its board in keeping with its own particular needs, objectives, and traditions. The adjoining diagram is suggestive.

In structuring the single board, some guiding principles may be helpful:

1. Each member should clearly understand his role.

2. In some churches, a few or all members of the board may have the help of subcommittees.

3. All members of the board may participate in serving communion, or else a special group of "deacons" may be appointed for this purpose.

4. Though some functions may be combined, "financial enlistment," which has responsibility for raising church funds, should not be combined with building maintenance and budget control. The kind of person who is skilled in conserving church assets is usually not the one to conduct the fund-raising program.

5. Sections of this manual which interpret the responsibilities of Christian education board members are relevant to the work of members of a single board who work in related areas.

6. If the functioning of a single board does not cover adequately all functions which should be carried on by a board of Christian education, then the members of the board who work in the educational ministry may wish to meet independently on occasion to care for the neglected functions.

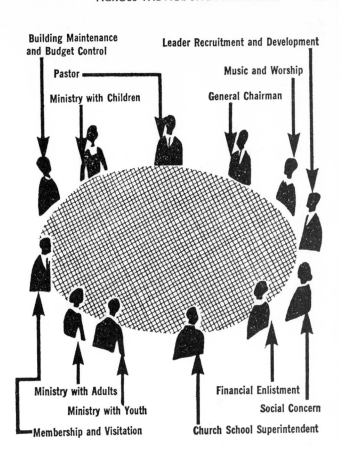

Building Maintenance and Budget Control
Pastor
Ministry with Children
Leader Recruitment and Development
Music and Worship
General Chairman
Ministry with Adults
Ministry with Youth
Membership and Visitation
Financial Enlistment
Social Concern
Church School Superintendent

Section 7 | Across-the-Age-Span Ministries

CHRISTIAN LEARNING is derived from the interaction between the gospel and the lifelong persistent concerns of the learner. The gospel comes alive and its meaning is recognized by the learner only when he sees it as relevant to his own life concerns. Since these concerns vary in form from year to year, depending upon the degree of one's maturity and the character of one's experiences, for educational purposes grouping together of persons with similar concerns, degrees of maturity, and life experiences is necessary.

With some exceptions, grading students on the basis of school experience has proven to be most satisfactory. Beyond the school years, grouping adults on the basis of approximate age has been customary. But there is a growing trend to arrange adult groupings on the basis of interests and concerns.

Within the past half century, a system of grading has been developed which is accepted by most denominations as the standard. It consists of three major divisions: children, youth, and adult, each of which is divided into subgroups or departments.

For many years, the primary, junior, junior high, and senior high departments included a cycle of three grades each. It was customary to maintain only one departmental grouping at each level, no matter how many pupils were enrolled. Thus a single department could have as many as fifty or seventy-five students. A more recent development limits the number in any one department or adult class and provides for multiple groups within departments and smaller adult classes when otherwise the groupings would be too large. Children's departments should not have more than thirty persons, and adult classes not more than fifteen. Many churches have developed two-grade departments, or if there are a sufficient number of students, single-grade departments at some or all age levels.

A church employing a three-grade grouping will have the following departments:

Children's Division

Nursery Department (birth to 3 years)
Kindergarten Department (ages 4 and 5)
Primary Department (grades 1, 2, and 3)
Junior Department (grades 4, 5, and 6)

Youth Division

Junior High Department (grades 7, 8, and 9)
Senior High Department (grades 10, 11, and 12)

Adult Division

Above high school

A church employing a two-grade grouping will have the following departments:

Children's Division

Nursery Department
    Crib Room (up to 12 months)
    Toddlers (1-year-olds)
    2's and 3's (Separate 2's and 3's if possible)
Kindergarten Department (ages 4 and 5)
Primary Department (grades 1 and 2)
Middler Department (grades 3 and 4)
Junior Department (grades 5 and 6)

Youth Division

Junior High Department (grades 7 and 8)
Middle High Department (grades 9 and 10)
Senior High Department (grades 11 and 12)

Adult Division

Above high school (does not follow a strict grading system)

Because of different numbers of students at different age levels, a church may use a two-grade plan of grouping in the children's division, and a three-grade plan of grouping in the youth division, or vice versa. Or a church may use a two-grade plan of grouping in the church school and a three-grade plan in the vacation church school.

In the adult division, persons of the same general age range have usually been placed in the same class. But there is a growing trend to structure the adult division on the basis of common interests or elective courses, in which case the matter of age is not particularly important, unless the nature of the course demands it, as a course for parents of young children or a course on preparing for retirement.

AGE-GROUP MINISTRIES

MINISTRY WITH CHILDREN

The earliest years are a critical stage in a person's life. Lasting impressions are made in this period; a basic sense of trust or distrust is developed. Here foundations are laid for future conscious relationships to God, to other persons, and to oneself.

Young children are especially receptive and respond strongly to the environment provided for their nurture. As they experience warm, satisfying relationships with understanding adults who love God, they grow increasingly in ability to trust God and to say "thank you" to him. As they experience love and forgiveness from sensitive, mature adults, they grow in ability to deal with their own feelings and to consider the feelings of others. For four- and five-year-olds the meanings of the gospel become real as they learn to forgive and to receive forgiveness. First and second graders can recognize the church as a fellowship of persons with needs to forgive and accept forgiveness, to love and to accept love and support.

The nursery child is becoming aware of himself as an individual separate from his environment and needs opportunities to express his feelings in a climate of understanding. His persistent "No" and "I can do it myself" are triumphant declarations of independence. The development of a wholesome self-image begins in the earliest years when the child begins to learn "I am important"; "I am loved"; "I am wanted"; "I belong"; "It's good to be me." Kindergarten and primary children live in an expanding world of friends and schoolmates, where they are confronted with the need to recognize the worth of others as well as their own.

The young child feels wonder at the mysteries of nature and is full of questions about life and death. He should have opportunities to explore his world through all his senses — seeing, tasting, hearing, touching, doing — and to feel love from secure adults who also view God's world with a sense of awe and wonder. In such experiences, prayer and an attitude of reverence for all life have their roots.

The Bible, which is the basic document of the Christian church, is recognized by young children to be a special and important book as they see it read and studied by their parents and other adults, as they learn that it is used in their church's worship, and as they learn that it tells about God and Jesus. They appreciate it as they hear the Bible stories which have meaning and value to them, especially those which help them know Jesus, who loved children and drew children to him. Primary children are excited about their new skills in reading, and they enjoy using Bible story books as well as verses and brief passages from the Bible.

The older child is moving out of the closeness of his family and is beginning to explore his rapidly enlarging world. He is less dependent upon adults as he discovers exciting possibilities in relationships with his peers and with history and science. However, he still needs the secure love and support of his parents and teachers, as well as their encouragement and guidance. He is growing in his desire and ability to relate meaningfully to other persons and he has a strong sense of justice. As the exciting world of juvenile books and television reveals to him the injustices of the world, he becomes aware of the need for his talents to be used in the service of others.

As he explores the wonders of the natural world, the older child learns how man is enabled to use its resources. He can grow in understanding God's creative action and come to know God more fully as Creator and Sustainer of the universe. He is a child of the scientific age and insists on knowing, "Is it true?" His increasing absorption with science may lead to questions and doubts about the Bible. Elementary children need secure, open adults who encourage their questions and are able to guide and to join them in their search for answers.

Elementary children can take a great deal of initiative for their own learning, and they need teachers who can present them with a variety of resources and encourage them to search for meanings. The creative teacher will see in their curiosity and sense of adventure a great challenge. These boys and girls can find the Bible very exciting as the source of adventures, struggles, and aspirations, and in such experiences they can see their own world, even their own lives and needs.

Middlers and juniors are developing skills in using the Bible and are growing in knowledge of the biblical world. As they study history and become aware of problems of the world, they are able to understand something of Jesus' world, the problems he faced, the spirit in which he faced them, and the meaning of his life to help them in living bravely and with compassion and love. Their interest in adventure and biography makes the story of Jesus' matchless life very appealing — and a challenge to affirm the meanings of the gospel for their own lives.

Ministry with Youth

The transitional period of the youth years is a composite of complexities and perplexities. The young person is trying to understand himself and the world around him. While the youth has a need for some dependence, adolescence is a time of search for self-identity and independence. The search for identity usually reaches a crisis during these years, and from this time on, adolescence becomes a period marked by reasoning

and an embodiment of a self-concept and a personal set of values.

Since adolescents are so significantly involved in achieving a sense of personal identity, the concern of Christian education for youth is basically a matter of accepting the gospel in the fullest sense. This means coming to an understanding of oneself and using one's system of values in dealing as a Christian with confronting problems. The church's educational ministry helps challenge youth to accept the full implications of the gospel.

Along with becoming a whole person, the adolescent is growing in his relationship to God. Youth may raise questions about God, but they are increasingly able to realize that this is God's world and to sense their own relationship to him. Youth begin to accept their responsibility in the world and to prove their love for God by loving their fellowmen.

Curriculum, to be relevant, must present the meanings and experiences of redemption. Youth experience loneliness, anxiety, alienation, sin, and guilt. They need to meet with God's forgiveness. They can best comprehend this by being in relationship with adults who understand what it means to forgive and to be forgiven. Youth are growing in a responsible and trusting relationship with others.

As youth explore their special concern about the meaning of life and vocation, they are searching for a personal understanding of discipleship. They are asking, "What then shall I do?" Appealing ideas call for experimentation.

In the curriculum for youth, all the learning tasks are undertaken, but personal appropriation of the meaning and value of the gospel in all relationships is a predominant learning task. While some of youth's appropriation of the gospel may seem superficial from an adult point of view, Christian education leaders must recognize that, in adolescence, the person for the first time has a whole self to dedicate.

The curriculum for the church's educational ministry with youth will include goals and activities for study, creative expression, fellowship, stewardship, service, and worship.

Ministry with Adults

Learners in the adult division are represented by a diversity of ages ranging from the post-high-school years to threescore and ten, and then some. Within this constituency are college students, single persons, married couples, homemakers, parents, widows and widowers, grandparents, the aging, the divorced, the homebound, the physically handicapped, and still others. The church's ministry of education must take into account both the needs of these persons and their potential contributions to the mission for which the Christian church exists.

Adults may be divided into three general categories: young adults, middle adults, and older adults. Each period is characterized by new experiences, new challenges, and new patterns of life.

Young Adults range in age from approximately eighteen to thirty. This is the period when persons are becoming adjusted to the routines and dailiness of life. Some young adults are much concerned with facing up to the responsibilities and demands of parenthood. In families where both work, parents face the problem of day care for their children. Those who have not married represent a sizable group, and the church should provide also for their needs. Young adults must develop a mature faith, must find ways of translating their youthful idealism into practical modes of expression. They need also to identify themselves responsibly with the ministry of the church, which can be particularly helpful to young parents in establishing meaningful practices and patterns of living in the home. Another basic need is an understanding of Christian stewardship by which they may develop a balanced expenditure of time and financial resources in meeting the needs of their home, the church, and the community.

Middle Adults represent the ages of approximately thirty to sixty years. This group includes the persons on whom the church depends most for its life and work. Middle adults are at the prime of their life and the peak of their vocational efficiency. Some will have achieved a degree of affluence and prominence and may wield considerable influence in the life of the community. Some will have suffered disappointments and deprivations with an attendant demoralizing effect upon their personalities. By the end of this period, middle adults will have launched their children into the world of economic independence and have reached the "empty nest" stage. They are likely to have marginal time available for significant service in the church and community, but this period is not without frustrations of its own. These persons are more fully aware that man is finite and that some of the ambitions of youth and young adulthood will remain unfulfilled.

Middle adults need a growing faith, lest they try to meet the demands of maturity with childish concepts and naive oversimplifications. They need acceptance and the ability to accept others. They can find such relationships through experiences of fellowship in groups where they are free to take off the mask of pretension and be themselves, and where they learn to know and to become sensitive to others as real persons. They need to understand the complex structures and the powerful forces in the life of the world in order to witness and serve intelligently within the social order. They need to understand what it means to be a Christian presence within the sphere that engages so much of their time, the area of their employment.

Older adults are persons over sixty years of age. The change from being a middle adult to an older adult is gradual. For some, it involves an increase in physical ailments, diminishing vigor, the avoidance of strenuous activity, and a generally more cautious and conservative attitude. Of course, there are notable exceptions. From Moses to Grandma Moses, there have been unusual persons who made their greatest contributions during the latter years of life. But, for most people, older adulthood will be accompanied by a slackening of the pace and a diminution of mental energy. For many, there will be retirement from their life work, a reduction of their mobility, drastically reduced income, and partial or even complete dependency.

Older adults need fellowship. Loneliness is one of the commonest by-products of aging. The older adult has been losing his old friends one by one and is probably not replacing them with the same number of new and meaningful friendships. The church can help him combat loneliness through a loving ministry which provides significant activities and companionship. The church can help him simplify his life and discover the things that are most important, useful, and meaningful in the light of his limited time and strength. The church can suggest or provide older adults with activities through which they can make the remaining years count. Many retired persons possess important skills that can be used in the ministry of the church. Never before did they have an abundance of time not preoccupied with the busyness of making a living. Older adults want some assurance that will overcome their anxiety about the end of life. They want to face the future without fear.

All adult groups should provide basic training and motivation for participation in meaningful service both inside and outside the church. Unfortunately there are some church groups like a person whom Martin Luther described as being all curled up within himself. A church school class should regard it as an honor, and not a threat, when one of its members is selected to become the teacher of another class. Adults should be encouraged to give active leadership in significant community organizations and to assist in projects which meet community needs, such as Head Start programs, nursery schools, hospital service, day-care centers, tutorial programs, coffee-house ministries, and visitation of shut-ins.

Section 8 | Planning the Curriculum of the Educational Ministry

THE SELECTION of curriculum resources used in departments, classes, and special interest groups and the correlation of all teaching/learning experiences constitute one of the most significant functions of the board of Christian education. It is important that board members take this responsibility seriously, making certain that teachers and group leaders not only utilize approved teaching resources, but that they have an adequate understanding of theological, biblical, and educational objectives.

In the past, the term "curriculum" has been equated with lesson "quarterlies." Today, lesson materials are called "curriculum resources," while the word "curriculum" is given a broader meaning. Our definition of curriculum is well-stated by Randolph Crump Miller:

"Curriculum," which originally meant a race course, is the path traversed by pupil and teacher in reaching a desired objective. . . .
The basic curriculum is the whole of life, but the term is normally restricted to learning experiences under some kind of control by a responsible institution. . . . "The curriculum of Christian religious education is the experience of the learner under guidance." [1]

Let us make a distinction among three different phrases in order to avoid ambiguity. The *curriculum plan* is the design that is developed to provide guidance for the teaching-learning situation. It is a blueprint to indicate what is intended to happen. *Curriculum resources* are the materials used in the teaching-learning situation, such as course books, teacher's guidance, multimedia pictures, maps, etc. *Curriculum* is the actual experience that takes place, or as Miller says, "the experience of the learner under guidance." In this sense, *curriculum* is identical with *teaching-learning experience*. The teacher, the pupils, the resources all make a contribution to the curriculum.

[1] Randolph Crump Miller, *Education for Christian Living*, 2nd ed. (Englewood Cliffs, N.J.: Prentice-Hall, Inc., © 1963), pp. 43-44.

THE CURRICULUM PLAN

The most important curriculum development among Protestant churches is the Cooperative Curriculum Project. This project was started in 1960 and completed in 1964. Sixteen denominations sponsored and participated in the work, and the total membership of these denominations represents the bulk of American Protestants. The product of their work together is represented by an overall curriculum design published in a massive volume, *The Church's Educational Ministry*. In 1964, eleven denominations who participated in the Cooperative Curriculum Project, along with five additional denominations, began a second cooperative project, to develop a plan for curriculum development, including taxonomies for the curriculum plan, implications for leadership development in the plan, and a comprehensive listing of biblical resources. This project was concluded in 1966 with the publishing of the volume, *Tools of Curriculum Development for the Church's Educational Ministry*. These two books have served, since their publication, as the basis for most curriculum development among Protestant churches.

Based upon the work of the cooperative projects, American Baptists developed their own curriculum design, *Foundations for Curriculum*, published in 1966. This design is the basis for all curriculum resources to be published or recommended by the American Baptist Convention and has been named "The Christian Faith and Work Plan." The first resources to be published as part of the Christian Faith and Work Plan were designed for use in the church school and were made available in the fall of 1969. Eventually, the Christian Faith and Work Plan will embrace other settings, such as the vacation church school, the family, outdoor education, and fellowship groups, with specific resources provided for each.

The Objective

The Objective of the Church's Educational Ministry is stated and interpreted in Section Two. The Objective indicates the intent of the educational process, the end toward which curriculum resources should aim and toward which the teaching-learning encounter should be directed. The Objective should not differ from the purpose of the entire mission of the church, but should reflect how education contributes toward that purpose. The Objective is comprehensive and is applicable to every age level and to the whole gamut of human experience. It is ultimate in that it can never be fully achieved by the learner. It is always out ahead, drawing him on to greater understanding and deeper commitment throughout the lifelong learning process.

The Objective has four purposes: (1) it describes the direction in which planned educational experiences should be moving; (2) it is the standard for selecting short-term goals; (3) it is the standard for determining procedures, for using methods that will implement and support the intended learning; (4) it serves as a means for evaluating the whole educational program, including the teaching-learning experience.

The Scope

The scope of the curriculum plan embraces the whole field of man's relationships and experiences. These are evidenced in a person's lifelong persistent concerns, such as self-image, interpersonal relations, sex, sense of destiny, survival, affection, usefulness, power, security, authority, trust, love, forgiveness, reconciliation.

The scope of the Christian Faith and Work Plan gives a place of preeminence to the gospel, that is, the good news of what God has done which offers man the clue to his existence, his redemption, and his life vocation. The heart of the gospel is that God loves and that his love is so magnificent and extravagant that men who are sensitive to God will respond with love. They will respond also with love for neighbor and even enemies. They will become extravagant in their love.

Because of the love of God, man lives under judgment and is in need of the gospel — God's redemptive action. Therefore, in planning what is to be taught and learned, the gospel is the crucial factor. The gospel must be explicit in the curriculum plan in order to shed light on man's whole field of relationships.

The gospel is firmly anchored in the Scriptures. Man gains insight into the gospel through his knowledge of the Bible, as he is informed and illumined by the Holy Spirit. Therefore the Bible is the basic foundation and guide which in various ways permeates the entire educational ministry of the church.

The gospel comes alive and is recognized by the learner as being relevant only when he sees the gospel in connection with his persistent lifelong concerns. Where the gospel and the meanings and experiences of life meet is called the "crossing point."

God calls all men to discipleship. When man hears the call, a response is inevitable, though this response may be one of acceptance or rejection. Man may be greatly tempted to reject the call and may view himself as the source of life's authority. However, when man responds to God in faith and love, he finds that light is thrown on all his relationships.

The curriculum plan deals with three dimensions of reality (1) the Christian experience of man under God (the divine dimension); (2) the Christian experience of man's relationship to man (the human dimension); (3) the Christian experience of man within the world (the natural dimension). Together, these dimensions of reality, in light of the gospel, comprehend the entire scope.

The Context

Context refers to the learning environment in which education takes place. The context of the curriculum is basically "Christian community" — the reality of fellowship among persons who own allegiance to Jesus Christ. The more a particular congregation can approximate the true nature of the church, the more effective its nurture and witness become.

The context of the curriculum embraces a variety of factors that come into play in the process of implementing the curriculum plan: the nature of the learners, the location of their meetings, and the administrative arrangements, such as leadership, grouping, resources, time available, equipment, evaluation, and supervision. The church going about its work is the context for its education. This education must be related to the entire life and work of the congregation in worship, preaching, counseling, healing, church administration, outreach, stewardship, Christian service, and social action. The curriculum undergirds and helps implement these acts.

With this emphasis upon Christian community as the context of the church's curriculum, recognition must follow that the nurturing work of God through the Holy Spirit is not confined to the church. The church witnesses to the Holy Spirit and the Spirit works in and through the church. The church can neither limit nor direct the work of the Spirit, but it can obstruct or facilitate man's response.

The Learning Tasks

The curriculum plan deals with teaching-learning in terms of "learning tasks" by which a learner becomes engaged in the experiences of the curriculum. The word "task" is used in the sense that it identifies a stage in the learning process, and there are five principal stages:

1. Listening with growing alertness to the gospel and responding in faith and love

This task recognizes the transforming power of the Holy Spirit in the learning experience. It requires a continuing sensitivity to ever-new disclosures of God within all the relationships of life. When God speaks, man is obligated to listen. Listening is not a passive experience; it means becoming engrossed in the gospel, vitally reacting to it. It leads to the other four learning tasks.

2. Exploring the whole field of relationships in light of the gospel

This task recognizes that the gospel is concerned with all of life. No area is exempt from its penetrating observation and judgment. None of our relationships, with others or with the world, is "out of bounds" for honest exploration in the light of the gospel.

3. Discovering meaning and value in the field of relationships in light of the gospel

The closed mind is inappropriate and self-defeating in a learning situation. Both pupil and teacher must be open to new meanings and values that may emerge from the teaching-learning encounter. These values will be examined, compared, and tested in light of the gospel.

4. Appropriating personally the meaning and value discovered in the field of relationships in light of the gospel

Learning is a process of becoming. This involves change, the person restructuring himself. Such change will be evidenced in the form of altered concepts, skills, attitudes, appreciations, and finally in a new style of life.

5. Assuming personal and social responsibility in light of the gospel

The full realization of the learning process is not accomplished until the learner voluntarily carries another's burden in love, or risks status, comfort, security, or even safety in obedience to the demands of the gospel. The learner should have opportunities for assuming personal and social responsibilities in manageable doses, and, facing the consequences, be conscious of the support of the Christian fellowship and the approval of God.

These five learning tasks are part of a single process. They are not to be regarded as necessarily sequential.

The first one — "listening to the gospel and responding in faith and love" — comprehends the other four and relates closely to the Objective. But the teaching-learning encounter is not complete until the learner has moved through all five tasks. Even then, the completeness can only be approximate, since the gospel makes ever-increasing demands and Christian learning is a lifelong process.

Suggestions for a workshop session dealing with the five learning tasks are included in the packet "Focus on the Teaching Ministry." *Education for Change*, by Joseph D. Ban, is a helpful book dealing with the philosophy underlying the Christian Faith and Work Plan.

CURRICULUM RESOURCES

The great majority of curriculum resources are published denominationally, either by single denominations or by several denominations with similar concepts. It is normal for churches to use the materials provided by their own denomination, but with additional materials as supplemental resources. Let us examine some of the resources available for use in various educational settings.

THE CHURCH SCHOOL

All denominations provide or recommend curriculum materials for church schools. Some denominations provide two or more curriculum series for the church school setting. In this way broader options are available to meet the diversity of needs and interests of the students, teachers, and administrators in a church school. For example, the American Baptist Churches provides three curriculum series with a suggested process, Individual Curriculum Planning, which helps a church choose the most appropriate resources from the three series for each class or department. The following questions may serve as helpful guides in determining which curriculum is most appropriate for your church.[2]

Are the objectives (or goals):
- Theologically and educationally acceptable?
- Clearly stated and consistent throughout the material?
- Supportive of the church's statement of purpose for the church school?
- Supportive of the church's concepts of mission?

Is the content:
- Biblically-based?
- Related to the needs, development, and experiences of persons at each age level?
- Helpful to persons in living out the objectives in daily life and conduct?
- Understandable to persons at each age level?

[2] Kenneth D. Blazier, *Building an Effective Church School* (Valley Forge: Judson Press, 1976), pp. 56-57.

- Free of racial, ethnic, and sexist bias?
- Reflective of racial and ethnic differences?
- Concerned both for changes in attitudes and actions and for the development of knowledge and skills?
- Specific in indicating desired changes in the thoughts, feelings, attitudes, and actions of students?
- Written in style and vocabulary suitable to each age level?

Is the teacher:
- Seen as a stimulator, enabler, guide, co-learner?
- Stimulated to creative thinking and planning?
- Provided adequate helps and resources?
- Helped to develop a mature understanding of the Bible and Christian doctrine?

Do the teaching methods:
- Reflect the best principles of how persons learn?
- Provide opportunity for students to be actively involved in learning experiences?
- Produce an informal, relaxed atmosphere for learning and growth?
- Encourage the creativity of students?
- Develop leadership?

Do the curriculum materials:
- Include supplementary teaching aids, such as pictures, filmstrips, etc.?
- Provide clear objectives/purposes for each session/unit?
- Clearly relate each session to the previous session(s) and to units?
- Give suggestions for evaluating student progress toward the objectives?
- Provide home materials to coordinate the teaching of knowledge and attitudes?
- Use print type and size of material suitable to each age level?
- Have good artwork and photographs suitable to each age level?

EVENING FELLOWSHIP GROUPS

Several denominations issue guidance material for fellowship groups to study. In some cases, resources for children and youth are in the form of reading magazines which are used by the group members, augmented by special helps for the leaders. In others, quarterly or annual resources are issued. At the adult level, a variety of elective materials are recommended.

THROUGH-THE-WEEK EDUCATION

The *Through-the-Week Series* is a set of curriculum materials designed for use by churches and church groups and published by the Cooperative Publication Association for the National Council of Churches. The unique purpose of this series is to help elementary, middle, and secondary students evaluate their school experiences from a Christian perspective.

The Through-the-Week Series offers five basic books which deal with the gospel and conflicting faiths, and with four areas of school studies viewed from a Christian perspective: history, the person, science, and society. The basic books are used as study resources for eleventh and twelfth graders and provide background for teachers of all grades. There are course books for grades one to ten, built on the basis of thirty-two sessions, providing study suggestions for the year.

Outdoor Education

Curriculum resources for resident camping are provided by various denominations.

Several day-camping resources are available and will provide guidance for day-camp directors.

Encounter Groups

Several denominations provide suggestions of resources for use in encounter groups. Changes are made frequently in order to include materials that are relevant to the contemporary situation. The elective principle is recommended so that themes can be selected that are particularly adapted for and meaningful to each group.

Training Resources for Church Membership

Some material that is valuable for training for discipleship and church membership is included in the regular curriculum series for the church school. Additional materials for specific classes in church membership are provided by each denomination with emphases that are peculiar to its own distinctives, policies, and traditions.

Further information regarding curriculum resources, including a copy of the appropriate prospectus, as available, may be secured from the regional or area director of Christian education in your own denomination.

Section 9 | The Recruitment and Development of Leaders

Curriculum resources, grading, space, equipment, and good organization will be ineffective if dedicated, trained leadership is lacking. The need for leader development is apparent when one considers that the average church school has an annual turnover of from one fourth to one third of its workers.

Let us consider a definition of leadership: leadership is the performance of a service by a person or a group of persons in such a way as to help them further the purpose for which their group exists.

We may draw several conclusions from this definition. First, leadership is not performed in isolation, but in relation to a group. The best leader is the one who can stimulate the group to its maximum performance in light of its essential purpose. Second, the leader's relationship to the group is that of servant, and therefore not one that is measured in terms of status or ability to manipulate the group. Third, leadership is not the same as holding office. Every member of the group who helps it to advance its objectives is performing a leadership role. Thus we may distinguish between the "designated leader" and the "voluntary leader." The most effective group is one which utilizes the leadership gifts of all of its members. This section of the manual will deal primarily with the discovery, recruitment, training, and involvement of the designated leader.

Discovering Leaders

How can we tell a potential leader when we see one? What are the factors that need to be taken into consideration?

The first consideration is the style of a person's life. A prominent American preacher once said that preaching is not preparing a sermon and delivering it; preaching is preparing a person and delivering that. We can make a similar application to teaching. The most important element in teaching is the life of the teacher. In recognition of this principle, the phrase "leader development" is tending to replace the older term "leadership development." The development of the person is even more important than the development of skills.

As we look for the kind of persons we want to assume leadership roles, the Objective may provide us with clues: Is he deeply aware of God and does he respond in faith and love? Does he seek to know who he is and what his human situation means? Is he growing in his relationship with God and with other persons? Is his life rooted in the life of the Christian community? Does he try genuinely to love in obedience to the will of God in all of his relationships? Does he have a strong sense of Christian vocation?

The second consideration is his basic competence. Does he have the gift of teaching? The apostle Paul points out in the twelfth chapter of First Corinthians that the Holy Spirit has given to each person a special gift. All of these gifts should be used in such a way as will further the whole ministry of the church. Some people have the gift of teaching. Some have the capacity to be administrators. Unfair to the person and disastrous to the ministry of the church is the assumption by someone of a leadership role for which he is not basically equipped.

A third consideration is a person's suitability for a particular leadership role. One who could give adequate leadership in an adult class may have no ability whatsoever to lead a group of kindergarten children. Or a person who would be less than qualified to counsel a Sunday evening youth group or conduct a junior choir might serve effectively as a member of a board of Christian education. Persons who have responsibility for selecting personnel should not only have data concerning people being considered, but also a clear understanding of the kinds of persons who are needed for specific responsibilities.

Probably half of the members in an average congregation have the basic ability to serve in some designated leadership capacity. But how does a church go about the important business of finding these people and discovering their capabilities? Obviously there should be a committee or task force which systematically secures the necessary data. Many churches make use of a personnel file that includes relevant data concerning each member. A 4" x 6" card for this purpose, entitled "Christian Service Enlistment Card," may be secured from the Judson Book Store (Valley Forge, PA 19481; Northern Baptist Theological Seminary, 670 E. Butterfield Road, Lombard, IL 60148; or 816 S. Figueroa St., Los Angeles, CA 90017).

Having all members fill out the recruitment card is not easy to do, but an attempt should be made to do it. This can be done through personal visitation, or by mail, or by utilizing a worship service for this purpose. Some churches have each new member fill out the card as part of the process of joining the church and of expressing their willingness to assume the responsibilities of church membership.

When a personnel-card file is maintained, a valuable practice is to make a duplicate file, one set of cards to be filed alphabetically, and the other set by classified sections, as "ministry with children," or "ministry with youth." This will save valuable time when looking for persons to fulfill particular leadership needs. In some instances persons have more than one kind of skill, in which case more than one extra card is needed. Care should be taken to keep such a card system up-to-date, as people grow and/or develop new skills and expertise.

RECRUITING LEADERS

After a person has been selected by the board for a particular leadership role, he should be interviewed in his home. Two persons should make the call, one representing the church as a whole — the pastor, the chairman of the board of Christian education, or the general church school superintendent — and the other representing the department or group to be served — the department superintendent, a teacher, or an age-group chairman.

The callers should be sensitive to the kinds of questions that the prospective leader will have in mind. What will be expected of me? Can I qualify for the job and satisfy people's expectations? With whom will I be working and to whom will I be responsible? What resources will I have to work with? Will someone show me how to use the materials? Who was my predecessor and how well did he succeed? For how long a term will I be expected to serve? How meaningful is the task, and how is it related to the basic purpose and ministry of the church? What training opportunities will be provided?

Some churches may rely upon the telephone, or mail, or a hurried conversation following a church service for extending an invitation to prospective leaders, but such contacts are never as personal, friendly, or satisfying as a personal visit. Visitors should take with them a sample of the resources to be used by the prospective leader, so that he may know the kind of printed and other helps that will assist him in performing his task. The task should be presented clearly and honestly, explaining what is expected of the leader. Coaxing and coercion should be avoided. If requested, time should be given for the person interviewed to consider the matter further, to pray about it, to "talk it over with my family." A second call may be necessary.

TRAINING LEADERS

All leaders within the educational ministry should have continuous training, just as long as they serve. Every leader needs to deepen his commitment to his Christian vocation, to keep alive to the meaning of his task, to sense fresh challenges, to share significant insights, and to develop greater competence in performing his task.

There are three areas in which a leader requires continuing education:

First, in the area of his personal growth. Every leader should experience a growing relationship with God, a greater understanding and appreciation of Christ, a stronger background in biblical theology, an authentic relationship with the church, enlarging insights on what it means to be a Christian in all relationships of his life, an openness and an ability to listen and relate to others.

Second, in the area of his task. Training will provide growing insights and experience in the performance of his particular responsibility. This will include a knowledge of the organization's structures and traditional procedures, its goals, programs, and emphases, and the use of available resources. It will include the technical know-how of methods and procedures through which goals may be achieved.

Third, in the area of group behavior. Usually, a leader has a relationship with a group, a class, a board, or a fellowship of his peers. It is therefore important that increasingly he learns how to contribute meaningfully to the group process and help make it effective. To do this, he must learn to understand the persons in the group as persons, the dynamic forces that are at work, and how to further communication and group goals.

RESOURCES FOR LEADER DEVELOPMENT

A large variety of training resources is available. Based upon its own particular needs, each church will use those which seem most appropriate.

FOCUS ON THE TEACHING MINISTRY

Guide for planning leader development. The book, *Enlist, Train, Support Church Leaders* by Evelyn M. Huber (Judson Press) is a valuable resource. It explains how a church can go about their leadership skills for a more effective ministry. It is a workbook for planning an overall strategy for the development of leaders.

The Annual Launch of the church school year. The purpose of the Annual Launch is to prepare the entire congregation to participate responsibly in the church school. This emphasis helps the church launch its church school year and prepare its leaders for their roles in the teaching-learning opportunities of the church school. A helpful resource is *Launching the Church School Year* by Kenneth D. Blazier (Judson Press).

Training events for teachers. The teacher is the key to the teaching-learning experiences of the church school. Consequently, administrators of the school seek ways to help each teacher grow in his understanding of himself, other persons, the gospel, and educational philosophy. Several denominations provide resources for training opportunities for teachers to be held in a local church setting.

> For further information on current leader development resources, write to the Division of Church Education, American Baptist Churches, Valley Forge, PA 19481.

CONSULTANTS

Persons are available in each city society and state/regional convention of the American Baptist Churches to serve as consultants to local churches regarding the philosophy, settings, resources, and leader development opportunities for Christian education.

In your area such persons may include:

• City, state, and regional directors of Christian education; professional persons serving with administrative responsibility for the educational ministry of a city, state, or region

• Members of city/state/regional committees or departments of Christian education; persons of competence in educational ministry who are elected to serve in a city, state, or region

• Other qualified persons with specialized skills

> For further information and to secure the services of such persons, contact your city, state, or regional American Baptist office.

CONVOCATIONS, CONFERENCES, WORKSHOPS

Training events for associations or clusters of churches are periodically conducted in city societies and state/regional conventions. These may include convocations and special conferences, such as institutes for vacation church school workers, workshops on group process, observation-demonstration days or weekends, and other training opportunities. Local, state, and national persons provide leadership for such events.

LEADERSHIP COURSES

Leadership courses and schools have been a traditional means of training educational personnel and are still used advantageously. An entire leadership curriculum plan has been developed to meet many kinds of leadership needs. Textbooks for the pupils and guidance for the teachers are available. Send to your denominational regional or area director of Christian education for information concerning these courses.

LABORATORY SCHOOLS

For most teachers and administrators, the laboratory school provides the most effective leader development opportunity. Laboratory schools are usually conducted for one or two weeks under the sponsorship of denominational or interdenominational agencies. There are specific laboratory schools for adult workers with children, youth, and adults. Many churches include an item in their budgets for sending selected persons to laboratory schools each year. It is recommended that churches send three or more persons to a laboratory school in any given year so they can be supportive of each other as they work together in their own church.

APPRENTICE TEACHING

An apprentice teacher may be assigned to work for a period of time with an experienced teacher. He observes the work of the experienced leader, who assigns some teaching responsibilities to him. With this kind of experience under supervision, an apprentice develops confidence and skill. Only highly competent teachers should be selected to provide this kind of guidance. Team teaching may have some of the values of apprentice teaching, as members of the team share in their work and learn from each other.

SUPERVISION

A qualified counselor is appointed by the board to observe teachers at work and counsel with them later on the basis of the observation experience. The counselor must be a person with recognized teaching skills who possesses great tact. He must be able to establish good rapport with the teachers being observed. The time for observation must be agreed upon in advance so that the teacher knows that the supervisor is coming and is not taken by surprise. The counselor never makes any suggestions during the teaching experience, but holds a conference with the teacher as soon as possible after the session is over.

RETREATS

Increasingly, churches are using weekend retreats in a camp or conference setting for leader development. Retreats may be conducted for human relations training under skilled leadership, for renewal seminars to consider one's Christian vocation in relation to the mission of the church, or to acquire leadership techniques.

CURRICULUM RESOURCES

Persons who use denominational curriculum resources know that much help is provided in the course materials. If the teacher studies his guidance material carefully, he will receive the benefit of a built-in course in the use of good teaching procedures.

ENCOUNTER GROUPS

In addition to participating in church worship experiences, every church leader should experience occasionally the fellowship of the church by participation in one of its small study or encounter groups. The group should be small (8 to 12 participants), informal, spontaneous. The purpose may be for study, for personal encounter, for deepening of the devotional life, or for action in the community.

PLANNING CONFERENCES

While containing some elements of a retreat, the planning conference concentrates on practical problems: the evaluation of the program, shaping up new plans, the correlation between programs, and the assignment of task responsibilities. The lack of time pressure (often on a weekend) and the informality of the situation can help persons understand one another better, develop morale within the staff, and sense a unity with the church and its mission.

GUIDED READING

Church leaders should be people who read, and some of their reading should be related to their task of communicating the Christian gospel. A carefully administered church library can provide church workers with significant reading opportunities. It is not only important to make good books available, but their use should be encouraged, and some guidance provided. Also, every church school leader needs to read one or more of the excellent religious and educational magazines which are published today.

The Committee and its Task

If there is a committee on leader development in the board of Christian education, its activities may include the following:

• Becoming familiar with the entire field of leader development

• Discovering the leadership needs of the church's educational ministry

• Discovering and recruiting leaders and recommending them to the board for appointment

• Developing and carrying out a long-range program of leader development

• Planning and arranging for the conduct of specific activities, such as leadership schools, courses, workshops, and retreats

• Supervising the library

• Recruiting persons to attend summer camps, conferences, and laboratory schools

• Providing the board with reports, including the evaluation of completed projects

---

For resources related to the recruitment and training of leaders, write to the Division of Church Education, American Baptist Churches, Valley Forge, PA 19481.

Section 10 | Education for Missions

As INDICATED in Section Six, "Structuring the Board," one member of the board of Christian education is recommended to be designated as chairman of education for missions. Historically, this person is a successor to the chairman of missionary and stewardship education, but as chairman of education for missions, he is given a broader assignment of responsibilities than characterized his predecessor. He still functions in the area of missionary and stewardship education, but his scope is enlarged to include some additional functions.

The word "mission" is derived from the Latin verb meaning "to send." The word "apostle" has a similar meaning. Mission is an essential characteristic of Christianity. No sooner had Jesus called the twelve disciples than he began to send them forth on missions. Again, he organized a group of seventy, trained them, and sent them on a mission. On the night that our Lord was betrayed, with only a few hours remaining to be with his disciples — time to say only the most important things — he prayed, "As thou didst send me into the world, so I have sent them into the world" (John 17:18). Still later, Jesus commanded his disciples to "Go therefore and make disciples of all nations, baptizing them in the name of the Father and of the Son and of the Holy Spirit, teaching them to observe all that I have commanded you" (Matthew 28:19-20).

The Great Commission expresses the basic spirit of the Christian movement. The church is to be an evangelizing, missionary fellowship. Christian educators are to be missionaries. A suggestion is, therefore, that one member of the board be commissioned to sensitize the educational leadership of the church to the evangelistic and missionary imperative of Christianity and the needs in the community and the world that call for a response in terms of a relevant educational ministry. Of course, all members of the board should exhibit this kind of concern, but they often become so enmeshed in the details of their own programs that they do not attend to "the weightier matters of the law." In addition, there are some concerns that need emphasis and implementation across age-group lines, and that the board as a whole may not recognize unless there is one member who accepts these concerns as a specific responsibility.

The Committee and Its Task

The chairman of education for missions should perform three functions:

First, help the board and its committees demonstrate an active concern for unreached persons in the community. This is in keeping with the Objective, "That *all* persons be aware of God through his self-disclosure." Within walking distance of every church there are persons who are not engaged in any type of religious learning experience. Many churches live from year to year with little recognition that these persons exist. Perhaps some of the unreached represent a different racial or economic background, and there may be church leaders who need a conversion experience before they will ex-

press any concern to bring them into church groups. From time to time, every church should conduct or join with other churches in conducting a community census and follow-up.

Second, help the board and its committees to understand the needs of the community and to develop teaching programs that are relevant to these needs. The chairman of education for missions should be a resource person who can provide pertinent information concerning the life of the community. What are the major problems in the school system? What inequities exist in the community that can be corrected? How is the welfare system working? What is the extent and what are the causes of delinquency? Are there adequate recreation facilities? What are the evidences of racism? Are there housing problems? Are there needs for tutorial services? What is the situation regarding alcoholism and drug addiction? These are the kinds of questions which church leaders should be asking and which could determine the content of some educational programs.

Third, help the board and its committees to be concerned about the Christian world mission and use effectively the missionary and stewardship education materials that are available. Excellent teaching-learning resources are prepared annually by the denomination, and by the National Council of Churches. The chairman of education for missions can be informed thoroughly about these resources and bring them to the attention of appropriate teaching personnel.

In the small church, the committee on education for missions may consist of four members: the chairman, and a representative of each of the age group committees, preferably the age-group chairmen. In larger churches, other members may be added, such as a representative from the youth fellowship(s), the men's fellowship, the women's society, and the chairman of the church committee on world mission support.

The committee on education for missions may include the following activities:

1. Initiating a program to discover and contact unreached persons in the community

2. Conducting a continuous study of the community to discover its needs and opportunities for service

3. Helping church groups become informed regarding pressing community needs with the expectation that forms of community witness and service will be developed

4. Promoting a church-wide program of reading in the fields of missionary and stewardship education and Christian social concern, including denominational magazines

5. Sponsoring a graded school of missions, and arranging for its effective administration

6. Helping to integrate missionary and stewardship education within the entire teaching program

7. Becoming increasingly knowledgeable concerning missionary and stewardship education and the many facets of Christian social progress

8. Establishing a contact with denominational missionaries and sharing information concerning their work

Section 11 | A Strategic Planning Model

STRATEGIC PLANNING is a synonym for long-range planning. It has to do with planning for programs that are five to ten years in the future, as contrasted with the regular year-by-year program planning.

The past twenty-five years have witnessed a whole new understanding of how an organization can plan effectively its future program. Leaders in the business world and social scientists have combined resources for the purpose of developing effective planning strategies. While these strategies may differ from organization to organization, they follow a basically similar pattern. A study of the strategic planning done by business corporations like IBM, large universities, and some national church organizations will reveal a remarkable similarity in design.

The planning model suggested in this section has been developed by the American Baptist Convention for use by national and regional agencies and by local churches. In its pattern, it is similar to models used by other denominations. A more complete description may be found in *Strategic Planning for Church Organizations*, by Richard R. Broholm.

Use of the strategic planning model is desirable as a total church project in which all boards of the church participate. Whether or not this is possible in any given situation, there is significant value for the board of Christian education to utilize the planning model in the projection of its own program. In some cases, the board of Christian education may be a pioneer and develop a planning pattern which the church as a whole may follow later. In addition to the value of the end results, there are educational values which will derive from the procedure as by-products.

A word of warning is in order: strategic planning requires considerable time and expertise. It will be almost impossible for a board to use this planning model unless it has someone working with it who has had experience in strategic planning and who can give guidance to the project—someone, perhaps, who has taken part in strategic planning in business or governmental organizations. The board may find such a person in the church membership, or it may coopt someone from the community to work with it for a year or two and help

it get under way. The project may be developed either by the board as a whole or by a specially appointed committee.

The strategic planning process includes the following steps, repeated over and over again: (1) clarification of assumptions, (2) specification of objectives, (3) development of strategies, (4) development of tactics, (5) review and evaluation.

1. Clarification of Assumptions

Any group can make progress more rapidly if its members share similar assumptions. Much of the controversy and conflict within groups could be avoided if the members could clarify and work from a common basis of assumptions. All the work of planning, whether strategic or immediate planning, will be expedited if the members of the board can agree upon their basic assumptions.

In order to undertake its mission, the church must listen to the world and to the gospel. Listening to the world makes it possible to define more clearly the needs which call the church to mission. Listening to the gospel makes it possible to define more clearly the nature of that mission.

Three types of assumptions are important: (1) the environmental assumptions list the most important things that we hear when we listen to the world; (2) the theological assumptions list the things that we hear when we listen to the gospel and that are most relevant to our environmental situation; (3) the operational assumptions list the characteristics of our organization which must be taken into account as we plan for the future.

a. Environmental assumptions

In a rapidly changing world, it will be necessary to take account of major changes. The shape of some of these changes can be deduced from our knowledge of present trends. Others will come into view only in the future. Since strategic planning is concerned about programming for the future—the next decade, for instance—it is necessary to anticipate what some of these changes will be. Areas in which changes should be noted may include: education, housing, recreation, the arts, social service, the economy, transportation, communication, ecology, government, the family, moral values, population characteristics, and a global approach to living.

In developing a list of environmental assumptions, the question should be asked, "What significant changes are likely to take place within the next decade?" Sample statements of environmental assumptions are: "There will be shorter work weeks, longer weekends, and longer vacations." "There will be increased housing and other services for the elderly." "Incomes will continue to grow and a nationally guaranteed annual income will be enacted."

b. Theological assumptions

Interpreting the gospel in order to understand its claims upon life is a constant imperative. Because it speaks of God's continuing work of redemption in human history, each generation must engage in the work of interpreting the gospel for itself, building upon the work of previous generations but never relying upon them exclusively.

A statement of theological assumptions does not need to include a complete systematic statement of theology, but rather particular theological assumptions that are relevant to the planning process. Some sample statements of theological assumptions are: "God is the creator of all life, but man is made in the image of God and shares with him in the continuing creative process." "The prophetic traditions of the Bible and the teachings of Jesus underscore God's special concern for the poor as well as the perils associated with the possession of wealth." "Insofar as the church is authentically the 'body of Christ,' it will live out a 'cruciform' existence in the world." "The church does not exist for its own sake. The kingdom, not the church, is the goal of God's redeeming activity."

c. Operational assumptions

Operational assumptions will answer the question, "What changes in the life of our church are likely to take place in the next decade?" This step represents an important transition between the consideration of environmental and theological assumptions, and the next step — the development of objectives. Our objectives, strategies, and tactics will be conditioned and limited by the character of the organization through which we do our work.

Some statements of operational assumption are: "Our church will accept increasing responsibility in meeting needs in our community." "Our young people will be challenged by what they see as relevant issues, rather than by appeals to institutional loyalty." "Our profes-

sional leadership, as well as our lay leadership, will require continuing education."

2. Specification of Objectives

In light of the needs of the world and the claims of the gospel, a church should specify its major objectives to be stressed during the decade for which the program is planned. These objectives should derive from or be related to the Objective of the Educational Ministry. They should be relevant to the statement of assumptions. They should clearly and simply state the specific purposes which the church hopes to achieve. A great deal of time should be spent on this statement, both in preparation and in constant review.

Some statements of objectives are: "To bridge the generation gap within the families of the church." "To give the younger laity a more responsible role within the life of the church." "To find ways of working with and serving needy residents in deprived communities." "To provide a more adequately trained teaching staff."

3. Development of Strategies

The course taken by congregations frequently has been as follows: first, decide what programs will be carried out; and second, state some of the objectives which these programs will accomplish. Obviously this is working backwards. In contrast, strategic planning is based upon the assumption that strategies and tactics must follow the choice of desired objectives. Action programs must be developed to achieve the objectives. In the course of carrying out a strategy, some objectives may be changed, and others take their place, but the church will always be clear about why it has made these changes.

To develop a strategy, it will be necessary to answer the following questions: What are the kinds of action needed? Can we secure the personnel to carry them out? What financial and physical resources will be needed? Who will have responsibility for making decisions about starting, changing, and terminating the project? It will not be possible to undertake all the strategies that can be developed; therefore, after examining alternatives, a clear choice of priorities will have to be made by the board.

If an objective chosen by the board is "to bridge the generation gap," then a related strategy could be "to conduct a series of four discussions for parents and their teenage children on various aspects of the generation gap, utilizing panels of both parents and youth." Or if an objective is to find ways of working with and serving needy residents in deprived communities, then a related strategy could be, for example, "to explore the possibilities of conducting a Head Start program in the community."

4. Development of Tactics

The tactics in the planning process are the practical steps to be taken in order to implement a specific strategy. They should describe in detail the proposed action, the specific persons involved, their role and assignment, and the target date when their work is to be accomplished, or when progress reports are to be made.

5. Review and Evaluation

Once the four preceding steps of the planning process have been designed, it may not be assumed that the work of planning has come to an end. Planning is a continuous process. All plans should be regarded as tentative and subject to review and change in the light of changing conditions. Two kinds of review and evaluation are called for:

a. Planning review

As objectives are stated, assumptions need to be reviewed in the light of the statement of objectives. As strategies and tactics are formulated, assumptions and objectives both should be reviewed to make sure that they are consistent with one another. There is always the danger that, having worked out the details of a planning design, the parent group shall consider its work final and definitive, treating each section of the finished project with a sanctity that it does not deserve. The repetitive character of the planning process must be emphasized continuously.

b. Program review

As programs are carried out, the effectiveness of the tactics must be reviewed periodically in the light of assumptions and objectives. Systematic evaluation is necessary to have even a proximate knowledge of whether the objectives are being achieved. A plan for evaluation should be developed as part of each proposed strategy. Additional suggestions regarding evaluation are included in Section Twelve.

Customarily planning is thought of as a straight-line process in which plans are successively developed, adopted, and carried out. Strategic planning is better understood as a circular process in which the results of each step modify all that has gone before and condition all that will take place in the future. In this way, strategies are continuously refined until it is possible to be increasingly specific about what they are able to accomplish and why. At the same time, allowance is continually made for new developments.

THE STRATEGIC PLANNING PROCESS

1. Clarification of Assumptions
2. Specification of Objectives
3. Development of Strategies
4. Development of Tactics
5. Review and Evaluation

Section 12 | Evaluating the Church's Educational Ministry

WHETHER or not the educational ministry of a church should be evaluated is not optional. The students, parents, teachers, and other program leaders pass judgment upon it from the point of view of what they believe an educational program ought to be. The entire church constituency judges the significance of its teaching program. What is being done informally ought to be done on a basis that is more objective, systematic, and relevant to the approved purposes of the church's educational ministry.

Evaluation is not a luxury. It is an essential prerequisite to progress. It provides information and guidance that is necessary if improvement is to be made. It develops a divine discontent with the inferior or mediocre, and creates the motivation that must be aroused if there are to be any changes for the better.

The Objective of the Church's Educational Ministry ought to be central in the minds of evaluators as they develop the criteria for evaluation. Let us look at some key phrases in the Objective and ask a few evaluative questions which they suggest.

"All persons"

Are we enlisting all church members as students in the educational program of the church?

What are we doing to reach the unreached persons in our community?

What are we doing about persons of different cultural levels or racial backgrounds?

Are we living to ourselves or are we sharing in a ministry that reaches persons in the inner city?

Are we showing a concern for the unreached in other countries?

"Aware of God"

Are we helping persons to know God, or only to know about him?

Are we providing meaningful experiences of worship within the educational program?

Are we helping persons discover where God is working in the world today?

"Respond in faith and love"

Have leaders of educational programs shown evidence that they are becoming more of a team, a community of love?

"They may know who they are," "Grow as sons of God"

What evidences of change in the lives of the learners can be observed?

What decisions and commitments have been made and carried out?

"Rooted in the Christian community"

How well do groups within the teaching ministry exhibit the characteristics of Christian community?

Have learners demonstrated new understandings of the church, more effective participation in its life?

Has the church shown a concern for persons in the educational programs and demonstrated its love in tangible ways?

"The will of God in every relationship"

Do the teachers have a clear concept of "crossing point" and are they helping their pupils to apply this principle in all of their relationships?

"Fulfill their common vocation in the world"

Is there a growing recognition of Christian vocation and the ministry of the laity?

Is the educational program helping the church to address itself to the needs of the community? Of the world?

There is another element of the curriculum plan which could serve an evaluative purpose, namely, the learning tasks (p. 29). They suggest some questions that could be useful in helping the teacher to check his teaching to ascertain whether he is using a good balance of procedures. Is he helping his pupils to

. . . Listen with growing alertness

. . . Explore

. . . Discover

. . . Appropriate meaning

. . . Assume personal and social responsibility?

PERSONAL SELF-APPRAISAL

In some of the curriculum resources, suggestions for evaluation are written into the course material. The class is asked to help set the learning goals at the start of the course. At its conclusion, learners are asked to evaluate their experience in the light of their established goals. This procedure has the advantage that students have a part in setting the goals upon which their experience is to be evaluated.

This principle — to assume a major role in setting goals for their own personal development — can also be used with leaders. This can be done by any person who has the determination to do it. Malcolm Knowles suggests four steps for developing such a program:

1. Build as specifically as you can a model of the kind of leader you want to be.
2. Identify the gaps between where you are now and where you want to be.
3. Identify the resources available to you for learning these competencies and then plan a strategy for making use of these resources.
4. Evaluate each learning in order to measure your progress and replan your strategy.[1]

While intended for use with adult group leaders, this strategy can be used equally well with groups of youth or adults. It can be used appropriately at the beginning of a church school year for setting personal goals and adopting plans for personal development by which these goals can be met.

APPRAISAL OF GROUP MEETINGS

All groups from later childhood up should take time occasionally to review their procedures and plan for improvement. With groups that meet only once a month, there may be value in doing this at every meeting. The procedure can be brief and simple, or on occasion more comprehensive. There are two principal ways in which meetings can be evaluated. First, evaluation can be done by one person. A member of the group possessing this kind of skill may be asked to evaluate the meeting and report his observations at the close. The group should be asked in advance to consent to the evaluation.

Or there may be someone outside the group, either in the church or in the community, who has special aptitudes in the whole field of group relations and who can serve as observer. Such a person should be allowed time, not only to give his reactions, but also to provide some education in group procedures as he explains assumptions about group behavior that lie back of his evaluations.

[1] By permission of Leadership Resources, Inc., 1750 Pennsylvania Ave., N.W., Washington, D.C. 20006, from the *Looking into Leadership Series*, Monograph 4, *The Leader Looks at Self Development* by Malcolm S. Knowles.

When one person does the evaluating, his observations should be made objectively, as a friendly observer who raises some questions with the group about what he has witnessed. He should not be an answer man who prescribes the cure; the group should be encouraged to do that for themselves.

A second procedure is to have the entire group participate in the evaluation. This kind of feedback is technically known as "postmeeting reactions," sometimes abbreviated to PMR's. The procedure may be brief and informal, the group being asked to respond to two or three simple questions, such as "At what points was our procedure most effective?" "Least effective?" "How could it be improved?"

Or the group may use a more comprehensive instrument. Models of evaluation scales are available in numerous source materials, such as the book by Philip A. Anderson, *Church Meetings That Matter* (pp. 50-52), or Martha Leypoldt's *40 Ways to Teach in Groups* (pp. 118-120). A study of other models is helpful, but a group will be more highly motivated to take their evaluation seriously if they develop their own instrument.

APPRAISAL OF GROUP PROGRAMS

This kind of evaluation has to do with groups that are responsible for carrying out some kind of program other than holding meetings or class sessions, such as church boards, age-group committees, women's societies, etc. Some program evaluation will take place in the normal functioning of the organization: as groups meet and study together, new insights will emerge which call for changes or improvements in the program. Such insights ought to feed immediately into the ongoing program and effect improvements. An annual program planning conference is a definite time when a degree of program evaluation is needed.

In addition to these ongoing experiences of evaluation, a more extensive evaluation of program elements in depth is needed. A major problem in carrying on this type of evaluation is that the educational ministry contains so many elements that need to be evaluated that it is impossible to deal with them all within a single year or even several years. Perhaps a plan should be developed by which particular aspects of the program would be evaluated each year. Over a given period of years, the entire program would be subjected to a careful, analytical scrutiny.

The following listing, adapted from an article by D. Campbell Wyckoff, suggests the various categories of program elements needing evaluation:[2]

[2] Adapted from D. Campbell Wyckoff, "Research and Evaluation in Christian Education," *An Introduction to Christian Education*, Marvin J. Taylor, ed. (Nashville: Abingdon Press, 1966), p. 152.

Purposes of the educational ministry
Administration: the board of Christian education; the officers and their duties; channels of communication
Organization of the participants; recruitment and attendance; grouping and grading
Curriculum plan and resources
Building, equipment, and supplies
Finance
Operational services: maintenance, audio-visuals, library
Public relations
The total ministry with children
The total ministry with youth
The total ministry with adults
Christian education in the home
Cooperative community services
Supervisory services
Leader development

We must avoid the kind of evaluation that becomes an end in itself. How many churches have made thorough and extensive evaluations of their programs and then done nothing about the results! Facts demanding drastic changes stared them in the face, but church leaders walked away from them as though they did not exist. To make a study of a church program and then do nothing about it is a sinful waste. We need to be conservative in our question-asking and use the data we collect. "What difference does it make?" is a question we must always ask.

STEPS IN PROGRAM EVALUATION

1. *Define the project.* Identify the area or program needing evaluation. Describe what needs to be evaluated, what kinds of questions need to be asked, and who will be responsible for administering the project.

2. *Agree to undertake the evaluation project.* After fully recognizing the demands that will be made upon time, energy, and possibly budget, decide to move ahead.

3. *Plan the schedule.* If the work will require the assistance of a substantial group of persons, the project must be scheduled well in advance so that the church can clear its calendar to avoid conflicts.

4. *Publicize the program.* If this is done early, it will enable other groups to avoid scheduling programs that will conflict. It will support the effort to recruit participants in the project — they will feel that the church is taking the matter seriously. It is not good to surprise people with evaluation. All participants should know what they are getting into.

5. *Enlist the participants.* Recruit the persons needed to carry on the project. This should be done well in advance.

6. *Clarify the goals.* The original purpose of the project should be reviewed and the goals should be stated more precisely. How do the stated goals compare with the objective and assumptions of the educational ministry? Are the goals stated in terms that lend themselves to measurement?

7. *Develop the design.* What pattern of activities will be followed? How will each step be accomplished? What are the dates for each design element? Who will do the work? What evaluative instruments will be used?

8. *Gather the data.* The kind of information desired will determine the manner of collecting the data. The gathering of partial data may lead to unreliable conclusions.

9. *Interpret the data.* This is fully as important as collecting the data. What are the correlations and patterns? Do the data indicate trends? What successes and strengths are discovered? What failures and weaknesses? What are the greatest needs revealed by the data?

10. *Make proper recommendations.* On the basis of the data, suitable recommendations should be developed: administrative procedures changed, new programs needed, old programs eliminated, additional personnel required, program goals restated, etc. After consideration by the board, recommendations should be presented to the groups or persons to whom they are relevant and who have the authority and the power to carry them out.

Section 13 | The Life of the Board

MUCH HAS BEEN learned about group process during the past quarter century, especially concerning the functioning of small groups. Since the board of Christian education is a small group, some of these new learnings can contribute to the life and work of the board.

Any group within the church should have three major functions: (1) the task function, (2) the development of the individuals within the group, (3) the group maintenance function. Let us examine the work of the board in the light of each.

TASK PERFORMANCE

The board of Christian education has been created by the church with at least a partial understanding of what such a board should do, and the expectation that it will do its job reasonably well. Whatever else the board may do, it must work at its appointed task. Its success will be measured by the quality of its achievements.

1. The board needs a common understanding of the reason for its existence.

No group can make satisfactory progress toward the achievement of its task unless a clear understanding of its purposes and goals is shared by all members of the group. Unless there is agreement at this point, board members will have difficulty working together. Each will have his own goal, and all will be working at cross purposes. The board will save time and probably some injured feelings if it starts with a clearly stated set of purposes which all members understand and with which they concur. This means more than adoption of the Objective of the Educational Ministry or its equivalent, although this is obviously necessary. It also means agreement regarding the responsibilities which the board will assume and the manner in which the board will operate.

2. An effective board does long- and short-range planning.

Too many boards live a hand-to-mouth existence. They spend all their time putting out fires because they failed to do the necessary planning that would have prevented the fire in the first place. In addition to strategic planning, discussed in Section Eleven, the board should conduct a yearly planning conference for determining annual emphases and activities. Such a planning conference should include other personnel in addition to board members, such as church school departmental superintendents or lead teachers, and key leaders of other educational programs in the church. Failing to do that kind of planning, a board simply reproduces what has been handed down from the past, with no effort to frame adaptations that are necessary to make the overall program relevant to today's world.

3. An effective board determines priorities.

There is always a temptation to spend valuable time and energy on nonessentials. There are so many things that can be done within the program of Christian education that a board can easily waste its time doing what is unimportant while significant needs remain unmet. This can happen if objectives and goals are inadequate. It also can result from planning that takes hold of the first idea which comes along, without examining and weighing alternatives.

4. An effective board has well-planned meetings.

Planning a meeting is not the sole prerogative of the chairman. The chairman must suggest important items that need to be considered from his own knowledge of matters that are pending and from advance contact with key members of the board. But he will always ask the board members to review the list, add other items, and approve the work list, determining what should be considered or given priority if time is not available for every item.

5. An effective board is a working board.

In a series of leaflets on group process issued by *Newsweek*, the news magazine, there is a suggestion that we do away with the word *agenda*. For its place, the phrase *work list* is recommended. The writer argues that *agenda* suggests the kind of experience where group members sit back and witness some proceedings that have been prearranged and which demand no involvement. On the other hand, *work list* makes it clear that work is to be done and that members are to be participants. Decisions are going to be made, actions are going to result!

But the work of the board must not be limited to what is done in monthly meetings. The meetings are necessary, for the purpose of planning the work of the board, but the effectiveness of the board is determined mostly by what happens between meetings.

6. An effective board completes its homework.

Many boards fail because members do not get their homework done. When this happens, board meetings get bogged down with details that are limited in their significance and not relevant to all board members. One board spent an hour and a half arguing about what kind of cabinets should be placed in the primary department and just where they should be located. This could well have been cared for by the chairman of ministry with children in conjunction with leaders of the primary department. If a board spends too much time on the administrative details, it will never deal with the really significant matters.

7. An effective board aims to achieve consensus.

Robert's Rules of Order is not helpful at this point. In order to discuss a question which involves making a decision, parliamentary procedure demands that a motion be made and seconded before the question can be discussed. But motions are then made before any aspects of the question have been considered, even by the person making the motion. Motions are therefore frequently faulty, inadequate in wording, ambiguous in meaning, or they may overlook important aspects of the question. Amendments are made to rectify the mistakes in the motion, and this may be followed by substitute motions and tangled procedures. Moreover, as soon as a motion is made, some people support the motion in its stated form and others oppose it. Instead of functioning as a fellowship in search of the most viable solution to a problem, the board may become divided into two opposing camps, each endeavoring to prove its point. When the motion is passed, some members have the feeling of being winners while others are losers. When the board comes to the task of implementing an action determined by such a procedure, there is no guarantee that those who voted against the motion will now rally to its support.

There is a better way. Let board members discuss a concern informally before anyone attempts to state a motion. Let them look at all possible solutions, examining the values and implications of each one. When someone senses that a consensus or near-consensus exists, he may then make a motion gathering up the most important elements growing out of the discussion. Or the chairman may state, "I believe that we have a consensus that. . . . Is that right?" The chairman should always receive some kind of response from the group to make sure that consensus really does exist. Where the matter under discussion is of great importance, a carefully worded motion is desirable.

Speaking to the desirability of procedure by consensus, LeRoy Judson Day says:

> Groups move and persons are changed by consensus and agreement, not by controversy. An emotionally charged discussion is not a good discussion, but many people fail to recognize the difference between argument and debate, on the one hand, and discussion on the other. In the former, the attempt is made to overpower the opposition in one way or another. The goal of the one who argues is to inflict his view upon another. . . . Discussion, on the other hand, is at its best a mutual sharing of information, understandings, and insights in a co-operative effort to solve a problem, reach a decision, or discover the truth.
>
> Through this process it is possible to come to a consensus, a unanimity of purpose which becomes the basis for concerted action.[1]

STIMULATING PERSONAL GROWTH

While members of the board of Christian education must as responsible members serve the board, the board also has a responsibility of serving them as persons.

[1] LeRoy Judson Day, *Dynamic Christian Fellowship*, rev. ed. (Valley Forge: Judson Press, 1968), p. 81.

Most boards fail at this point. Their concern for the accomplishment of tasks is so great that they fail to recognize the personal needs of their members. Let it always be remembered that people are more important than programs!

The member of a board of Christian education who is not a growing person is an anomaly. He is a member of a board whose basic business is to help people grow, and yet he is not growing. But the board can be and should be an instrument for the growth of every one of its members.

1. The effective board can help members be real persons.

The Swiss psychiatrist-theologian Paul Tournier makes a distinction between a "person" and a "personage." By "person," he means the person as he really is. By "personage," he means the image that a person creates in the minds of others. Generally a person wears a mask that conceals the real person and makes him out to be something other than he is, a "personage." Only when one possesses considerable trust in another, or in a group of persons, will he dare to remove his mask and be himself.

There are fewer and fewer situations in life where persons have the kind of trust relationships that make them free to take off their masks and let others know them as they really are. The board of Christian education should be such a group, and to the extent that it is, it can render a real contribution to the lives of its members. Everyone needs the experience of sharing in a group whose members he can trust and who will respond to him as he really is. From such fellowship comes the ability to develop an authentic self-image, to answer truthfully the question, "Who am I?"

2. The effective board develops one's ability to communicate.

Informality and flexibility are the spirit of an effective board. The members do not sit in straight rows with the chairman behind a table. Instead, members are able to look at one another, note facial expressions and gestures, feel relaxed and free to participate in face-to-face discussion. Members of the board call each other by first names. When an issue is being considered, members are not required to address the chair, "Mr. Chairman," and then wait to be recognized. Instead, each person takes part in the discussion when he has something to contribute. The chairman does not interrupt this kind of "participatory leadership," except to keep it on the track and to call for consensus. Members learn to communicate through practicing communication. They learn to reveal their thoughts and feelings clearly and to avoid the kind of ambiguities which cause communication failures.

3. The effective board teaches its members the art of listening.

In his book, Church Meetings That Matter,[2] Philip Anderson indicates three levels of listening. The first level is to hear with our ears. We hear the words but do not enter fully into their meaning. We may not give them much attention because we are too busy thinking up what we are going to say next. The second level is to hear with our minds. Here we try to understand the content of the other person's words and analyze them rationally. The third level is to listen with the heart. We pay strict attention to what the other person is saying, without criticism or a feeling of personal superiority, but with love. We try to understand his feelings as well as his ideas. We put ourselves in the other person's place and really see what he is saying from his point of view. Really to hear the one who is speaking is to affirm him as a person, and to contribute to his sense of personal worth.

4. The effective board pays attention to personal needs.

Every member comes to board meetings with personal needs. As he participates in the life of the group, he will betray these needs by the way he acts or through something he says. Others can develop their sensitivities to the point where they can recognize these needs and respond in ways that will help.

What are some of these personal needs? There is the need for acceptance, for being wholeheartedly trusted by the group, for being wanted, a need for feeling that one belongs. There is the need for security, for overcoming fear and distrust, the need to feel comfortable in the life of the group. There are other needs: mental stimulation, variety, a sense of meaning, the need for release from guilt feelings, and many more.

As LeRoy Day says:

If our groups are to operate effectively, they will have to take the needs of individual members into account and in some way integrate the meeting of those needs with the goals of the group. If our groups do this, we may speak of them as person-centered groups.[3]

5. The effective group provides training for its members.

Recognizing the need for growth and training, many boards utilize a portion of their regular meetings for specific training experiences. This may include studies in such areas as "The Mission and Ministry of the Church," "What Constitutes Good Teaching," "Community Problems that Need Our Attention," "The Meaning of the Objective of the Church's Educational Ministry," "the Annual Perspective Resources." "Effective Group

[2] Philip A. Anderson, Church Meetings That Matter (Philadelphia: United Church Press, 1965), pp. 28-29.

[3] Day, op. cit., p. 59.

Process," etc. There is value in having all members read a common study book, using meeting time to discuss what has been read.

In addition to studies conducted in regular meeting time, do not overlook the value of retreats held for a full day, or over a weekend. These can provide opportunities for seminars in depth, or human relations training under professional leadership.

GROUP MAINTENANCE

This has to do with the structure, inner workings, and other factors related to the board's maintaining itself as a group. There are housekeeping details that must be cared for. There is the further problem of maintaining the "groupness" of the board so that it is more than a conglomeration of persons trying to get some work done.

1. An effective board maintains an authentic meeting schedule.

Unlike many other church groups, the board of Christian education does not have to consider plans for adding new members — after all, it has a fixed membership determined by the church. However, it frequently faces the problem of having a full attendance at meetings. There are two factors that may help solve this problem.

First, there should be a regular meeting night, such as the second Monday, or the fourth Thursday of the month. When meeting dates are changed from month to month, it is easy for members to forget the date, or fail to record it in their calendars.

Second, meetings should start and end on time. The board members should determine the hour to start as well as the hour of closing. Members who are prompt are frustrated when forced to wait fifteen to forty-five minutes for others to arrive. And some members will resent it if meetings drag on toward midnight when they expected to get home by ten-thirty.

2. An effective board conducts meaningful meetings.

Most boards have one or more members who have gained some competence in the field of group relations,

through either church or nonchurch channels. Such a person may be requested to guide the board in developing improved procedures. From time to time, board members will be attending workshops dealing with group procedures, and upon their return they may be asked to share their newly acquired insights with the board. All members can be encouraged to attend workshops on group process or human relations seminars as opportunities are available.

3. An effective board will plan for a regular evaluation of its process.

At the end of board meetings, time should be allowed for evaluation, an appraisal of the meeting by one or more members of the group. How was the meeting helpful? At what points did the group proceed most effectively? Where did it bog down? Was there good participation? Did one or more members dominate the meeting? Did members listen to one another? Were all members accepted, or was anyone rejected by the group? Were discussions marked by honesty and an expression of feelings as well as ideas? Were there effective outcomes which may reasonably be expected to bear fruit?

Clues to evaluational procedures are indicated in Section Twelve. Evaluation must be handled with extreme care and tact until the board has become sufficiently mature (honest and accepting) to face procedural problems without becoming defensive or threatened.

4. An effective board is a manifestation of redemptive fellowship.

Like all groups within the church, the board should exhibit the churchly characteristic of being a fellowship of the Holy Spirit. The most important contribution that a board can make is to demonstrate to the church what a Christian fellowship is really like. This it can do if it continually tries to be aware of God's presence, seeking in all of its work to accomplish his purposes and develop a loving and trusting relationship with one another. Blessed is the board that becomes a fellowship in which the Spirit of God is present, recognized, and listened to.

ADMINISTRATION

Baptist Leader (monthly magazine of American Baptist Board of Education and Publication).

Blazier, Kenneth D., and Huber, Evelyn M., *Planning Christian Education in Your Church*. Valley Forge: Judson Press, 1974.

Bower, Robert K., *Administering Christian Education*. Grand Rapids: Wm. B. Eerdmans Publishing Co., 1964.

Broholm, Richard R., *Strategic Planning for Church Organizations*. Valley Forge: Judson Press, 1969.

LEADER DEVELOPMENT

Geyer, Nancy and Noll, Shirley, *Team Building in Church Groups*. Valley Forge: Judson Press, 1970.

Huber, Evelyn M., *Enlist, Train, Support Church Leaders*. Valley Forge: Judson Press, 1975.

GROUP PROCESS

Anderson, Philip A., *Church Meetings That Matter*. Philadelphia: United Church Press, 1965.

Day, LeRoy J., *Dynamic Christian Fellowship*, rev. ed. Valley Forge: Judson Press, 1968.

Leypoldt, Martha, *40 Ways to Teach in Groups*. Valley Forge: Judson Press, 1967.

TEACHING-LEARNING

Swain, Dorothy G., *Teach Me to Teach*. Valley Forge: Judson Press, 1964.

MINISTRY WITH CHILDREN

Write to the Department of Ministry with Children, Educational Ministries, A.B.C., U.S.A., Valley Forge, PA 19481, or to your denominational headquarters requesting the titles of current books or manuals related to the administration of ministry with children, teaching/learning opportunities, and curriculum resources for children.

MINISTRY WITH YOUTH

Write to the Department of Ministry with Youth, Educational Ministries, A.B.C., U.S.A., Valley Forge, PA 19481, or to your denominational headquarters requesting the titles of current books or manuals related to the administration of ministry with youth, teaching/learning opportunities, and curriculum resources for youth.

MINISTRY WITH ADULTS

Write to the Department of Ministry with Adults, Educational Ministries, A.B.C., U.S.A., Valley Forge, PA 19481, or to your denominational headquarters requesting the titles of current books or manuals related to the administration of ministry with adults, teaching/learning opportunities, and curriculum resources for adults.

CHURCH SCHOOL SUPERINTENDENT

Blazier, Kenneth D., *Building an Effective Church School*. Valley Forge: Judson Press, 1976.

Jones, Idris, *The Superintendent Plans His Work*. Valley Forge: Judson Press, 1956.

9621